JORGE LUIS BORGES

SELECTED POEMS 1923-1967

JORGE LUIS
BORGES

SELECTED POEMS 1923-1967

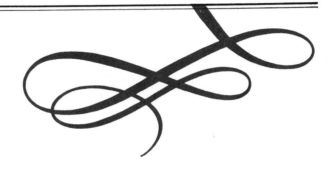

Edited, with an Introduction and Notes, by

NORMAN THOMAS DI GIOVANNI

A BILINGUAL EDITION

DELACORTE PRESS / SEYMOUR LAWRENCE

Assistance for the editing and translating of this volume was
given by the National Translation Center, the Center for
Inter-American Relations, and the Farfield Foundation.

LIBRARY OF CONGRESS CATALOGING IN PUBLICATION DATA
Borges, Jorge Luis, 1899–
Selected poems, 1923–1967.
"A Seymour Lawrence book."
English and Spanish.
Bibliography: p.
PQ7797.B635A17   1972   861   70–164850

THE TRANSLATORS

BEN BELITT

NORMAN THOMAS DI GIOVANNI

ALAN DUGAN

WILLIAM FERGUSON

ROBERT FITZGERALD

JOHN HOLLANDER

RICHARD HOWARD AND CESAR RENNERT

W. S. MERWIN

ALASTAIR REID

MARK STRAND

JOHN UPDIKE

RICHARD WILBUR

CONTENTS

AUTHOR'S FOREWORD   XV

INTRODUCTION   xvii

FERVOR OF BUENOS AIRES

Unknown Street   3

Sepulchral Inscription   5

Patio   7

Empty Drawing Room   9

Rosas   11

Remorse for Any Death   15

Inscription on Any Tomb   17

Afterglow   19

Daybreak   21

At the Butcher's   25

Plainness   27

Parting   29

MOON ACROSS THE WAY

Anticipation of Love   33
General Quiroga Rides to His Death in a Carriage   35
Manuscript Found in a Book of Joseph Conrad   37
Dulcia Linquimus Arva   39
Houses Like Angels   41
My Whole Life   43
Sunset Over Villa Ortúzar   45

SAN MARTIN COPYBOOK

The Mythical Founding of Buenos Aires   49
Isidoro Acevedo   53
Deathwatch on the Southside   57
Deaths of Buenos Aires   61
To Francisco López Merino   69

THE SELF AND THE OTHER

Two English Poems   75
The Cyclical Night   79
Conjectural Poem   83
To a Minor Poet of the Greek Anthology   87
A Page to Commemorate Colonel Suárez, Victor
    at Junín   89
Matthew XXV: 30   93
The Dagger   95
Compass   97
A Poet of the Thirteenth Century   99
A Soldier of Urbina   101
Limits   103
A Saxon (A.D. 449)   107

The Golem 111

Poem of the Gifts 117

Chess 121

Elvira de Alvear 125

Susana Soca 127

The Other Tiger 129

Allusion to a Shadow of the Nineties 133

Allusion to the Death of Colonel Francisco
    Borges (1833–1874) 135

The Borges 137

Embarking on the Study of Anglo-Saxon Grammar 139

Luke XXIII 141

Ars Poetica 143

A Rose and Milton 145

To One No Longer Young 147

Odyssey, Book Twenty-three 149

To a Minor Poet of 1899 151

Texas 153

Poem Written in a Copy of Beowulf 155

Hengest Cyning 157

Fragment 159

To a Saxon Poet 161

Snorri Sturluson (1179–1241) 163

To Charles XII of Sweden 165

Emanuel Swedenborg 167

Jonathan Edwards (1703–1758) 169

Emerson 171

Edgar Allan Poe 173

Camden 1892 175

Paris 1856 177

Rafael Cansinos-Assens 179

The Enigmas 181

To My Reader 183

Someone   185
Everness   187
Ewigkeit   189
Oedipus and the Riddle   191
Spinoza   193
Adam Cast Forth   195
To a Coin   197
Another Poem of Gifts   199
Ode Written in 1966   205
Lines I Might Have Written and Lost Around 1922   209
Junín   211
A Soldier Under Lee (1862)   213
The Sea   215
A Morning of 1649   217
To a Saxon Poet   219
The Labyrinth   221

FOR THE GUITAR

Milonga of the Two Brothers   225
Milonga of Albornoz   229

MUSEUM

Quatrain   235
Limits (or Good-byes)   237
The Poet Tells of His Fame   239
The Generous Enemy   241

APPENDICES

 I: New and Unreprinted Poems   245
 II: Prose Pieces from El hacedor   255
 III: Prefaces and a Dedication   267
 IV: Supplement of 1969 Revisions   281

NOTES   287

CONTENTS OF THE PRINCIPAL EDITIONS OF
    BORGES' POETRY   313

INDEX OF SPANISH AND ENGLISH TITLES   325

FOREWORD

First and foremost, I think of myself as a reader, then as a poet, then as a prose writer. The initial part of this statement calls for no explanation; the other two should be qualified. They do not mean— they emphatically do not mean—that I am fonder of my verse than of my prose, or that I judge it as technically better. For all I know, the opposite may be true. I suspect that poetry differs from prose not, as many have claimed, through their dissimilar word patterns, but by the fact that each is read in a different way. A passage read as though addressed to the reason is prose; read as though addressed to the imagination, it might be poetry. I cannot say whether my work is poetry or not; I can only say that my appeal is to the imagination. I am not a thinker. I am merely a man who has tried to explore the literary possibilities of metaphysics and of religion.

My stories are, in a sense, outside of me. I dream them, shape them, and set them down; after that, once sent out into the world, they belong to others. All that is personal to me, all that my friends good-naturedly tolerate in me—my likes and dislikes, my hobbies, my habits—are to be found in my verse. In the long run, perhaps, I shall stand or fall by my poems.

Goethe, who is not one of my heroes, thought that all poetry is occasional poetry (*Gelegenheitsdichtung*). I have forgotten the context, but I suppose his statement is open to at least two interpretations: he may have been apologizing for the all-too-plentiful verses he contributed to albums, or he may have implied that true poetry springs from what a particular man feels at a particular time. In my case, I can fairly claim that every piece in this book had its origin in a particular mood, in a necessity of its own, and was not meant to illustrate a theory or to fill out a volume. I have never thought of my poems, in fact, in terms of publication.

When this book was begun, some three years ago in Cambridge, it was the first time I had ever taken a direct hand in the translation of any of my own work. Di Giovanni and I have gone very thoroughly over each piece, each line, and each word; the fact that I am not only a collaborator but also the writer has given us greater freedom, since we are less tied to verbal precision than to inner meanings and intentions. I should like to thank the outstanding British and American poets who, by their skill and generosity, have made English poems of my Spanish originals and so given them this new life.

JORGE LUIS BORGES

Salt Lake City, March 31, 1971

INTRODUCTION

This is the first systematic presentation in English of the poems of a writer who made his initial fame in his own country nearly fifty years ago with his poetry, but whose present-day universal acclaim happens to rest on the small body of his prose. Until now, in England and the United States, we have known only the Borges of the puzzling short stories and luminous essays, Borges the brilliant conversationalist, the imitated Borges, the Anglo-American Borges. Of course, there is only one Borges, and no one will deny that the central vision which informs all his work is a poetic vision, but with a broad selection of the poems available we at last begin to have Borges whole. We may in this book even have, for the first time, the essence of Borges—the Borges who is one of South America's, and the world's, best poets.

Borges' poetry requires no special key. For those who like a biographical context, it is sufficient to point out here that the author was born in Buenos Aires, in 1899, learned English as a child at the side of an English grandmother, and came to poetry in English under the influence of his father, who loved England's great poets of the last century. Educated in Geneva during the First World War, where he discovered Whitman and the German expressionists, Borges began writing poetry in French and English. Later, in Spain, in 1919, he published his first poem, became involved with an imagist sect called the "ultraists," and, after returning to Buenos Aires, saw his first book into print himself. It would be superfluous to repeat in any greater detail what Borges has already told us about his early life and first writings in his recent short autobiography. (That essay, which is printed elsewhere, is not only a perfect introduction to Borges, setting his entire lifework in a frame, but also makes an ideal supplementary introduction to the present volume.) For the rest, Borges himself provides the most valuable insights into his own poetry; mindful of this, ten of his prefaces are included at the end of this edition, along with a full set of notes that furnish the reader with helpful historical and biographical information.

As a poet, Borges has striven over the years to write more and more clearly, plainly, and straightforwardly. A study of the revisions of his early work from edition to edition of the poems shows a stripping away of baroque ornament and a greater concern for natural word order and for the use of common language. Even his ideas about metaphor have moved in this direction. "When I was a young man," Borges has remarked, "I was always hunting for new metaphors; then I found out that really good metaphors are always the same." The emphasis, then, has been away from callow, tiresome, and merely clever inventiveness (a trolley car seen as a man shouldering a gun) to the stressing of familiar and natural affinities, such as dream-life, sleep-death, and the flow of rivers and time—a turn, as Borges bitingly terms it, to sanity. There is a great deal of truth to Borges' insistence that he has been first a reader and then a writer. For it is as a peruser of books that he constantly plumps for such unabashedly old-fashioned qualities as readability, pleasure, and enjoyment, demanding in turn that the writer in him provide this same complement of unacademic and refreshing virtues in his own work.* All these elements add up, I find, to endearing aspirations in a twentieth-century poet.

* Many of Borges' current views on poetry are found in three concise essays—"On the Classics," "A Defense of Poetry," and "The Metaphor"—collected under the title "Up from Ultraism" and published in *The New York Review of Books,* XV, 3, August 13, 1970.

I want now to introduce the present selection.

Jorge Luis Borges came into my consciousness in the fall of 1967. I was living an hour or so north of Boston, and I had been asked to compile a bilingual anthology of Latin-American verse. Reading Borges then for the first time in order to choose his best half-dozen pages, I quickly discovered several poems I admired, but I was most moved by a piece called "Elvira de Alvear," for something back of its lines—even in a weak translation—connected me straightaway with Borges' humanity. I couldn't have been greener, having come to Borges not through the celebrated stories but through the (then) overlooked poems. Wanting to learn more about the poet and the man, I next read Ronald Christ's intelligent Borges interview in the *Paris Review*. The author leaped alive and bristling off those pages—and yet modest and lovable and curiously self-effacing. I recognized the same Borges who had written "Elvira de Alvear." By that point, the English versions I had been reading all felt pale; the man who spoke with such sparkle and wit had to write far better than his translations showed. (His own English, I later found out, surpassed that of the general run of his translated work.) A study of the original texts became unavoidable, and, in Cambridge one day to buy them, I learned by chance that Borges was at Harvard at that moment and for that year as Charles Eliot Norton Professor of Poetry. Seizing this opportunity, I wrote him at once, proposing an English-language edition of his poetry, and he answered, asking me to pay him a visit. That visit, made early in December, 1967, has never ended. Borges and I liked each other, we enjoyed the work, and it was the right hour to have come knocking. At the time, Borges was suffering from an unhappy private life and from the peculiar isolation it had forced him into. I had happened along, all unwittingly, to help fill those long empty Sundays he so dreaded, to offer him the kind of work he could give his mind to (this in turn earned him much-needed self-justification), and to lend him the ear he desperately required. Ironically, in the short space of three weeks or a month, I had become the last American to discover Borges and the first to work with him. It was a lucky chain of events, and it kept getting luckier. Our project received the assistance of foundations, we were asked to organize a Borges reading in New York, and magazines began to take notice of what we were doing. The next April, before we parted, Borges invited me to come to Buenos Aires, and he also gave me carte blanche to handle all his publishing affairs in English. Six months later I rejoined him, and now for the past two and a half years I have been living in Buenos Aires, where Borges and I are producing English versions of twelve of his books. What started with that barely more than casual first reading has turned into a friendship, a trust, a whole career. "What I liked about you, di Giovanni," Borges confided to me on my arrival in Buenos Aires almost a year after we first met, "was that there at Harvard you were the only person who took me seriously as a poet." "But I see you as a poet, Borges." "Yes," he said, "I see myself as a poet—that's our link." So much for autobiography, so much for the hand of destiny.

The editing of this book was largely done in collaboration with the author. The choice of poems was worked out jointly. No very rigid principle of selection was necessary, since we were out to include as many poems as possible, but we did try to strike certain balances. We wanted to include all the famous poems, to cover every period, to represent most of the different forms and kinds of lines the poet has attempted, as well as to display his various thematic interests. At the same time, it seemed appropriate to print as many poems on American and Anglo-Saxon subjects as we could; these latter were of particular interest to me. Overall, of course, we favored the later poetry. Borges chafed and fussed a good deal over the choice of poems from his first three books, which he continues to improve with revisions but which nonetheless still cause him embarrassment, but with insistence and persistence I was finally able to convince him that much of this early work is both valuable and pleasurable. Over a third of the early pieces are in our selection and more than half of the author's later production. The ninety poems in the main section of this book represent slightly more than half the entire contents of Borges' *Obra poética 1923–1967,* from which our selection is drawn. We have also, in the appendices, included twelve additional pieces. In all, this book contains 102 poems, with 101 accompanying Spanish texts (one of the poems was written in

English). We hope in future editions to have the opportunity to expand the contents of the main section.

While the selection was being made, I went about choosing poets and commissioning translations. I began with six poets I had worked with before on a book of Jorge Guillén's poems (W. S. Merwin, Alastair Reid, Mark Strand, Richard Wilbur, Alan Dugan, and Ben Belitt); around Cambridge, I ran into Robert Fitzgerald, William Ferguson, and John Updike; later I was introduced to Richard Howard, who in turn introduced me to John Hollander. Everyone was keen on Borges, and no one had to be asked twice. Of existing translations (that also coincided with titles we wanted in our book), only the previous work of two poets seemed worthwhile. Robert Fitzgerald, who back in 1942 was responsible for Borges' second appearance in English, was asked to revise six of his early efforts, and Alastair Reid was called on to revise seven of his. Apart from these thirteen, everything else was especially prepared for this volume.

As the commissions and correspondence proceeded, a method began to evolve. This method was based on two factors: the difficulty of the poem and the translator's familiarity with Spanish. To begin with, on my own, I studied each poem and for most of them wrote out literal versions which I took to Borges and, because of the degree of his blindness, read to him. I would read a line or two of Spanish at a time, followed by an English equivalent for literal sense. Occasionally, my preparations exhausted, we wrote out trans-literations on the spot. Finally we had one prepared for every piece in the selection. On the sheets of these rough versions I also jotted down whatever deliberate or spontaneous comments on the poem Borges would make as I read it to him, and noted any additional biographical or historical background that came up in our talks. I was always on the lookout for particulars of local atmosphere—anything, in short, that I might pass on to the prospective translator in hopes of lightening his task or of improving the quality of the translation or of doing both. It was here and in this way that I tried to anticipate the translator's problems and his possible questions, and so solve them for him in advance. I made a point, for example, of telling a translator ahead of time which sense of *"sueño"* Borges intended in any given instance—"sleep" or "dream." (Because of the almost automatic connection between Borges and dreams, the unguided translator plumps unfailingly for "dream," yet more often than not the author's intention is "sleep.") There were also cases of Borges' sometimes idiosyncratic usage: throughout his work, the word *"tarde"* is rarely "afternoon" and usually "evening." (There is no afternoon in Buenos Aires, explains Borges; people sleep a siesta through the hot hours, and life only picks up in the evening.)

Poets whose knowledge of Spanish was little, or nonexistent, or out of practice received line-for-line and word-for-word transliterations, together with any other aids—such as notes, suggestions, or sources—that Borges and I could give. Those with a superior knowledge of Spanish usually got no literal versions but all the other help. However, where passages were exceptionally difficult, as in so much of Borges' early poetry, these hard lines might be spelled out word by word. Certain of the poems were not only very difficult but were also so local in topic that on two occasions Alastair Reid, whose Spanish is good, agreed to make translations only if I would provide the literal version worked out with Borges, plus whatever notes we could supply. One result of this is Reid's brilliant "Mythical Founding of Buenos Aires," a poem so compounded of local references and jokes—indeed, the whole poem is a joke—that at the same time we placed the raw material into the translator's hands, Borges and I tried to dissuade him from even attempting the task.

The degree of collaboration between Borges, editor, and each poet varied widely from poem to poem. Some pieces—especially Borges' later work, either on universal themes or else on subjects with which the translator felt at home—were brought into English with hardly an assist from Borges and me. Of course, the literal version was always there in my hands as a check. Other times—when the text presented difficulties or obscurities—several drafts and a long flow of letters went back and forth between poet and editor before a satisfactory version was reached. Usually, during these intermediate stages, I did not consult Borges—not until my own critical resources were exhausted. When at last I brought him a draft, it was either finished or close to being finished. As these results were read to him, Borges listened eagerly and was generous in his praise, often interrupting me to declare a line "far better than the original." It was always on the quality of the verse as it developed in English, and never on any jealous preservation of the Spanish lines or wording, that Borges focused his attention. In fact, so far was he from treating the Spanish originals as sacred text that many times Borges referred to his poems as "mere rough drafts" for the English versions. At the outset, he had even admonished me, "When you write to the poets, tell them that despite my poems the translations must be good."

There was a generous return from the poets, too. Many encouraged and some blessed our adopted method, and along the way I was helped and taught a good deal. Alan Dugan, in criticizing a few of my own translations, showed me that, despite my access to Borges, slips could be made and that I could not always be cocksure about my interpretation of knotty passages. This forced me to double-check with Borges thereafter whenever any phrase was not absolutely plain. John Updike complained, when I was being too literal-minded about one of his sonnets, that I had blithely ignored the fact that his lines were carefully composed in iambic pentameter. He was right. This awakened me to one sensible solution—and the one most widely adopted in the book—to the problem of treating Borges' sonnets in English. Following Updike's lead, I encouraged other translators to attempt blank verse, closing when possible with a rhymed couplet. Alastair Reid and I favored this example, since it does not force rhyme, which is not poetry. (Reid and I were to carry on a voluminous correspondence, useful to me, in which we discussed every angle of translation theory and practice.) Richard Wilbur, William Ferguson, and Robert Fitzgerald found their own ways with the sonnet form, as did John Hollander and Mark Strand. Richard Howard, who in César Rennert had a personal Spanish expert, applied to the form his favorite metrical scheme—syllable-count. His success tempted me in this direction, and I used syllabic meter to solve three different kinds of problems in translations of my own.

In the work of revising certain of their previous Borges translations, Robert Fitzgerald's and Alastair Reid's generosity knew no limits. I should like to give some detailed examples of the kinds of problems faced in the present book, and I may as well begin with illustrations from a pair of fresh versions undertaken by these two poets. Reid's "A Page to Commemorate Colonel Suárez, Victor at Junín" was first published in Anthony Kerrigan's edition of *A Personal Anthology*. There, although the tone and language were right, the poem was mysteriously missing a line, and it contained a number of annoying petty mistakes; worst of all was the confusion that resulted from the translator's lack of the hard (and complex) historical facts needed to set the action straight. Of course, without that proper tone in the first place, no amount of revision would have improved the poem; the essential background information Borges and I could supply. In the poem, Colonel Suárez, though an Argentine officer, was not living in his own land in alienation (as in Reid's first version), but was in exile in Uruguay; hence it was not luck but fate that took him there. In exile, time did not flow for him, but was a monotony. The battle itself was fought in the Andes, on a tableland in Peru—a place not to be confused with the Argentine town named for it at a later date. These were the Wars of Independence, and Suárez was leading Peruvian troops, not fighting against them. In one line, Borges had written simply of the *"laberinto de los ejércitos"* ("labyrinth of armies"), taking it for granted that his readers already knew that the engagement, so famous in South American history, was fought entirely between horsemen. No poet writing in English could be expected to be aware of this from Borges' Spanish. As here the translator was to change his earlier "foot soldiers" to "cavalries," with the rest of the biographical and historical details before him Reid went on to rework the central elements of the poem so as to make its sources in remote South American politics absolutely clear. Thanks to his gifts, not to mention his forbearance, the resulting new poem has gained in strength and vividness.

Robert Fitzgerald was invited to revise "Deathwatch on the Southside" (in its earlier life called "The Night They Kept Vigil in the South") for an entirely different set of reasons. To begin with, Borges had made numerous small revisions in the text since Fitzgerald had first translated it over twenty-five years before, and we wanted the English version to conform with these alterations. At the same time, with the author himself available for consultation, it seemed a good idea to try to clear up several vague or obscure points so characteristic of Borges' early style. First off, Borges revealed that the *"Sur"* in the title meant specifically the south side of Buenos Aires and did not refer to the south of Argentina or stand for some abstract symbolic South. But just what did he mean in one of his lines by *"el tiempo abundante de la noche"*? This was found out, passed on to Fitzgerald, and eventually the earlier "the abundant night-time" was transformed into "time grown pure in plenitude of night." Similarly, Borges' very difficult and subjective line *"y algún silbido solo en el mundo"* went from "a whistle alone in the world" to "and a whistler somewhere, lonely in the nightworld." Elsewhere, attending to the smallest details, Borges suggested that the word *"patio,"* which occurs frequently in the poem, not be rendered as "courtyard." To Borges this word evoked something far more magnificent than the humble patio he remembered from forty years earlier, when the events in the poem took place. Fitzgerald's simple and effective solution was "yard." It is in the almost impenetrable density of the poem's last eight lines, however, that Fitzgerald crowned his achievement. Exactly what was meant by *"sentenciosas calles del Sur"*? Borges saw at once that he had not really made his intention clear here, so he began shedding light on the text and giving me material for notes to send the translator. It seemed that the author meant "sententious" in a purely physical and descriptive sense. There was a terse and concise quality about the streets, and to describe them a word was required that would give the idea of long vistas and straight lines, of an unending sweep of the eye. Taking characteristic pains and working the poem through several drafts, Fitzgerald turned his earlier lines,

> and sententious and slowly-to-be-merited streets of the South,
> the dark breeze across the forehead that turns back,

to:

> and graven streets on the Southside, one by one to be savored,
> and a dark breeze in my face as I walk home.

My own translation of "Conjectural Poem" started out as an attempt to correct the errors and to relieve the literalness of two previous English versions of what is often considered Borges' finest poem. Each of these earlier translations had somehow dropped the same line, and one contained a disastrous error of meaning. But still worse was their diction: both gave "The lateral night" for the beginning of Borges' line *"La noche lateral de los pantanos"* (what in the world is a lateral night?), and one had rendered the simple Spanish word for "knife" as "poniard blade." Once I got beyond this objective of my translation, I felt myself already half-way into Laprida's hunted skin, and I just kept on in pursuit of physical sensations—from those cinders hailing down on the wind at the outset to the taste of metal at the end. Along the way, I got Borges to amplify the term *"montoneros"*—gaucho militiamen—and I scoured Dante for the reference to the *Purgatorio,* finding that Borges' fourteenth line is a direct translation from the Italian. When I put the question of "lateral night" to Borges, however, he astonished me. He said he no longer knew exactly what he meant. No pompous explanation, no defense, just that plain admission. Then, telling me to seek some satisfactory solution of my own, he went on to set that particular scene for me as he himself had conceived it after reading contemporary reports. Laprida had been overtaken on a kind of roadway, perhaps an embankment road, that cut through the marshland. It seemed to me, then, that Laprida would have felt the night pressing in from the swamps on either hand. Yes, said Borges, that was it; and there I had the kernel of my English line. Sometime later, when I was about to read a provisional draft of the poem's last section to Borges one afternoon, he interrupted to say that I ought to know beforehand that he had originally thought out part of one line in English and then translated it into Spanish. It was the half-line *"se ciernen sobre mí"*; his English phrase was "loom over me." Undaunted, I then read him my translation, "tighten the ring around me," which impressed him so favorably he quickly pronounced it better than his own. After this, spurred on by his open mind and generous spirit, I went back again to the beginning of the poem, wanting now to work it out in a metrical form. Unrhymed Spanish eleven-syllable lines in most cases can be turned into good English blank verse. In this poem, pentameter somehow seemed too rigid, so I shifted instead to a syllabic meter and shaped each line into ten syllables—a fitting solution, I think, since it allows freedom from measured stresses while still imposing on the lines a subtle restraint.

The making of Ben Belitt's translation "Deaths of Buenos Aires," one of Borges' longest poems and also his most difficult, exacted the heaviest demands on both the resources and the application of the three collaborators. At the outset, there seemed hardly a dozen lines in the poem that did not require the fullest explanation and note-gathering. Borges himself fretted, and he mocked his overly complicated and unnecessarily arduous early style. He no longer recalled the meaning of the word "*trapacerías*," for example, and sent me to the dictionary to find out. "Why can't a young poet's language be simple and straightforward?" he wondered. During one period, Borges confided to me, he had laid his hands on a dictionary of Argentinisms and worked in so many fancy local words that his own countrymen barely understood him. Over the years, though, through revision, much of this language had been set straight. When at last I wrote Belitt about the poem, I sent him two packed pages of notations. These included everything from pointing out the chief distinguishing features of the two cemeteries—the rather humble Chacarita and more dignified Recoleta—down to the meaning of unusual words like "*trapacerías*" and "*estrafalarias.*" Additionally, "*La Quema*" was not a symbolic Flame but the name of the municipal incinerator; "*suburbio*" was not what we mean by "suburb" but referred to the shabby, run-down outskirts of the city. And so on. Belitt, who found the poem to his taste, and a true challenge, then took over. His first draft was remarkably good; it was exciting and had set the proper tone. And yet I was to send him four pages of queries and criticisms (and praise), line by line. We set local geography straight, clarified images, and sought ever greater precision in word choice. The "tenements deep in the south" of his first draft became "the Southside's clustering tenements." Even punctuation was argued and defended back and forth through a long series of letters. A complete second draft invited more quibbles and produced more criticism. Finally, I read the poem to Borges, who felt as I did that it was a tremendous job. "Thanks for the joint blessing," wrote Belitt; "I was just about to throw in my sweaty old towel." There was a final flurry and round of tinkering. It had taken three months to bring the poem to its final stage, and I shared the translator's relief. In "Deaths of Buenos Aires," Belitt has produced a poem of undiminished power, and I think he has given us a masterpiece of translation.

A word, in conclusion, about the Spanish texts. Since the final onset of his blindness in the 1950's, Borges has been unable to exercise control over the proofreading of his work. From that time on, with each successive printing of his poems, while mistakes were occasionally caught, fresh errors usually crept in. Even a recent effort on our part to set this right was doomed to failure when the author and I could not be present in Buenos Aires to check final proof of all the volumes of the latest edition of his poetry. For the present selection, we have made every effort to correct past errors, and we have also incorporated or otherwise noted all of the author's most recent alterations. Many of the texts have been collated with their earliest printings in an effort to restore the correct placement of stanza breaks. At least one poem here is printed whole for the first time since 1954; a missing line had passed undetected through six subsequent different editions and several other reprintings. As well as to present Borges the poet in English, then, it has been an aim of this edition to perform the additional service of providing readers with accurate texts of the Spanish originals.

NORMAN THOMAS DI GIOVANNI

Buenos Aires, March 15, 1971

JORGE LUIS BORGES

SELECTED POEMS 1923-1967

I do not set up to be a poet. Only an all-round literary man: a man who talks, not one who sings. . . . Excuse this little apology for my muse; but I don't like to come before people who have a note of song, and let it be supposed I do not know the difference.

The Works of Robert Louis Stevenson,
Vailima Edition, XXII, 42 (London, 1923)

FERVOR OF BUENOS AIRES

[FERVOR DE BUENOS AIRES]

1923

CALLE DESCONOCIDA

Penumbra de la paloma
llamaron los hebreos a la iniciación de la tarde
cuando la sombra no entorpece los pasos
y la venida de la noche se advierte
como una música esperada,
no como símbolo de nuestra esencial nadería.
En esa hora de fina luz arenosa
mis pasos dieron con una calle ignorada,
abierta en noble anchura de terraza,
mostrando en las cornisas y en las paredes
colores blandos como el mismo cielo
que conmovía el fondo.
Todo—honesta medianía de las casas austeras,
travesura de columnitas y aldabas,
tal vez una esperanza de niña en los balcones—
se me adentró en el vano corazón
con limpidez de lágrima.
Quizá esa hora única
aventajaba con prestigio la calle,
dándole privilegios de ternura,
haciéndola real como una leyenda o un verso;
lo cierto es que la sentí lejanamente cercana
como recuerdo que si llega cansado
es porque viene de la hondura del alma.
Intimo y entrañable
era el milagro de la calle clara
y sólo después
entendí que aquel lugar era extraño,
que toda casa es candelabro
donde arden con aislada llama las vidas,
que todo inmeditado paso nuestro
camina sobre Gólgotas ajenos.

UNKNOWN STREET

Twilight of the dove
the Hebrews called the beginning of evening
when the shadow does not mire the footsteps
and the coming of night is recognized
like an awaited music,
not as a symbol of our essential insignificance.
In that hour of fine sandy light
my footsteps found a street I did not know
opening as though
onto a noble sweep of terrace,
disclosing on cornices and walls
colors as soft as the sky itself
that moved the background.
Everything—frank mediocrity of the plain houses,
playfulness of little columns and knockers,
perhaps a girl's hope from the window railings—
entered my vain heart
with the clarity of a tear.
That may have been the one hour
ever to enhance the street with a spell,
giving it privileges of tenderness,
making it real like a legend or a verse;
what is certain is that I felt it remotely near,
like a memory which arrives exhausted
only because it has come from the depths of the soul.
Miracle of the glowing street,
intimate and deeply stirring;
and only afterward
I realized that that place was strange,
that every house is a candelabra
where the lives burn each in its separate flame,
that each of our unthinking footsteps
makes its way over the Golgothas of others.

                                        [*W. S. Merwin*]

INSCRIPCION SEPULCRAL

Para el coronel Isidoro Suárez,
mi bisabuelo

Dilató su valor sobre los Andes.
Contrastó montañas y ejércitos.
La audacia fue costumbre de su espada.
Impuso en Junín término venturoso a la lucha
y a las lanzas del Perú dio sangre española.
Escribió su censo de hazañas
en prosa rígida como los clarines belísonos.
Murió cercado de un destierro implacable.
Hoy es un poco de ceniza y de gloria.

SEPULCHRAL INSCRIPTION

For Colonel Isidoro Suárez,
my great-grandfather

His valor passed beyond the Andes.
He fought against mountains and armies.
Audacity was a habit with his sword.
At Junín he put a lucky end to the fight
and gave Spanish blood to Peruvian lances.
He wrote his roll of deeds
in prose inflexible as battlesinging trumpets.
He died walled in by implacable exile.
Now he is a handful of dust and glory.

[Robert Fitzgerald]

UN PATIO

Con la tarde
se cansaron los dos o tres colores del patio.
La gran franqueza de la luna llena
ya no entusiasma su habitual firmamento.
Patio, cielo encauzado.
El patio es el declive
por el cual se derrama el cielo en la casa.
Serena,
la eternidad espera en la encrucijada de estrellas.
Grato es vivir en la amistad oscura
de un zaguán, de una parra y de un aljibe.

PATIO

With evening
the two or three colors of the patio grew weary.
The huge candor of the full moon
no longer enchants its usual firmament.
Patio: heaven's watercourse.
The patio is the slope
down which the sky flows into the house.
Serenely
eternity waits at the crossway of the stars.
It is lovely to live in the dark friendliness
of covered entrance way, arbor, and wellhead.

[*Robert Fitzgerald*]

SALA VACIA

Los muebles de caoba perpetúan
entre la indecisión del brocado
su tertulia de siempre.
Los daguerrotipos
mienten su falsa cercanía
de vejez enclaustrada en un espejo
y ante nuestro examen se escurren
como fechas inútiles
de borrosos aniversarios.
Con ademán desdibujado
su casi-voz angustiosa
corre detrás de nuestras almas
con más de medio siglo de atraso
y apenas si estará ahora
en las mañanas iniciales de nuestra infancia.
La actualidad constante
convincente y sanguínea
festeja en el trajín de la calle
su plenitud irrecusable
de apoteosis presente
mientras la luz
abre un boquete en los cristales
y humilla las seniles butacas
y arrincona y ahorca
la voz lacia
de los antepasados.

EMPTY DRAWING ROOM

Amid the brocade's dimness
the mahogany suite continues
its everlasting conversation.
The daguerreotypes tell their lie:
a false nearness
of old age cloistered in a mirror,
and when we look hard they elude us
like pointless dates
of murky anniversaries.
With a blurred gesture
their anxious almost-voice
runs after our souls
more than half a century late
and there it's scarcely reached
the first mornings of our childhood.
Actuality, ceaseless,
ruddy, and beyond doubt,
celebrates in the street's traffic
its unassailable abundance
of present apotheosis,
while the light
slices through the windowpanes
and humbles the senile armchairs
and corners and strangles
the shriveled voice
of these ancestors.

[*W. S. Merwin*]

ROSAS

En la sala tranquila
cuyo reloj austero derrama
un tiempo ya sin aventuras ni asombro
sobre la lastimosa blancura
que amortaja la pasión roja de la caoba,
alguien en queja de cariño
pronunció el nombre familiarmente horrendo.
La imagen del tirano
abarrotó el instante,
no clara como un mármol en un bosque,
sino grande y umbría
como la sombra de una remota montaña
y conjeturas y memorias
sucedieron a la mención eventual
como un eco insondable.
Famosamente infame
su nombre fue desolación en las calles,
idolátrico amor en el gauchaje
y horror de puñaladas en la historia.
Hoy el olvido borra su censo de muertes,
porque son parciales los crímenes
si los cotejamos con la fechoría del Tiempo,
esa inmortalidad infatigable
que anonada con silenciosa culpa las razas
y en cuya herida siempre abierta
que el último dios habrá de restañar el último día,
cabe toda la sangre derramada.
No sé si Rosas
fue sólo un ávido puñal como los abuelos decían;
creo que fue como tú y yo
un azar intercalado en los hechos
que vivió en la cotidiana zozobra
e inquietó para felicidades y penas
la incertidumbre de otros.

ROSAS

In the drawing room's quiet
whose rigorous clock scatters
its unclouded and ordinary time
on the desolate white
that swathes the mahogany's red heat,
a voice, reproachful and tender,
pronounced that familiarly sinister name.
Straightway his tyrannical image
loomed huge on the moment,
not like marble profiled by a forest,
but shadowy, vast, and remote
like a darkening mountain.
Conjecture and memory
flowed in on that casual utterance
like a bottomless echo.
Famous in infamy,
his name once could ravage a city,
rally the gaucho's idolatry,
and stab horror in history.
We lose count of those corpses today,
crime is more piecemeal
if we weigh Time's ferocity into the balance—
the unwearied immortality
that decimates men without ever declaring its guilt,
the festering wound
where all a world's bloodshed awaits the last of the gods
to seal the world's sores on the last of all days.
Perhaps Rosas
was only the implacable butcher our grandfathers
    thought him;
I think of him now, like ourselves, as
a creature of chance enclosed in an action's parentheses:
he lived out the everyday anguish of things
and for better or worse troubled
the age's uncertainty.

Hoy el mar es una separación caudalosa
entre sus restos y la patria,
hoy toda vida por lastimera que sea
puede pisar su nada y su noche.
Ya Dios lo habrá olvidado
y es menos una injuria que una piedad
demorar su infinita disolución
con limosnas de odio.

Today an ocean's span divides
what is left of his bones from his country;
today, grief-stricken or dry-eyed, the living
may grind both his night and his nullity under their heels.
Even God has forgotten him,
and to delay his eternal extinction
for a pittance of hatred
is to turn our contempt into charity now.

[*Ben Belitt*]

REMORDIMIENTO POR
CUALQUIER DEFUNCION

Libre de la memoria y de la esperanza,
ilimitado, abstracto, casi futuro,
el muerto no es un muerto: es la muerte.
Como el Dios de los místicos,
de quien deben negarse todos los predicados,
el muerto ubicuamente ajeno
no es sino la perdición y ausencia del mundo.
Todo se lo robamos,
no le dejamos ni un color ni una sílaba:
aquí está el patio que ya no comparten sus ojos,
allí la acera donde acechó su esperanza.
Hasta lo que pensamos
podría estarlo pensando él también;
nos hemos repartido como ladrones
el asombroso caudal de noches y días.

REMORSE FOR ANY DEATH

Free of memory and hope,
unlimited, abstract, almost future,
the dead person is not a dead person: it is death.
Like the God of the mystics,
whom they insist has no attributes,
the dead person, everywhere no one,
is nothing but the loss and absence of the world.
We rob it of everything,
we do not leave it one color, one syllable:
here is the yard which its eyes no longer take up,
there is the sidewalk where it waylaid its hope.
Even what we are thinking
it might be thinking too;
we have shared out like thieves
the amazing treasure of nights and days.

[*W. S. Merwin*]

INSCRIPCION EN CUALQUIER SEPULCRO

No arriesgue el mármol temerario
gárrulas infracciones al todopoder del olvido,
rememorando con prolijidad
el nombre, la opinión, los acontecimientos, la
    patria.
Tanto abalorio bien adjudicado está a la tiniebla
y el mármol no hable lo que callan los hombres.
Lo esencial de la vida fenecida
—la trémula esperanza,
el milagro implacable del dolor y el asombro del
    goce—
siempre perdurará.
Ciegamente reclama duración el alma arbitraria
cuando la tiene asegurada en vidas ajenas,
cuando tú mismo eres la continuación realizada
de quienes no alcanzaron tu tiempo
y otros serán (y son) tu inmortalidad en la tierra.

INSCRIPTION ON ANY TOMB

Let not the rash marble risk
garrulous breaches of oblivion's omnipotence,
in many words recalling
name, renown, events, birthplace.
All those glass jewels are best left in the dark.
Let not the marble say what men do not.
The essentials of the dead man's life—
the trembling hope,
the implacable miracle of pain, the wonder of sensual
    delight—
will abide forever.
Blindly the willful soul asks for length of days
when its survival is assured by the lives of others,
when you yourself are the embodied continuance
of those who did not live into your time
and others will be (and are) your immortality on
    earth.

[*W. S. Merwin*]

ULTIMO RESPLANDOR

Siempre es conmovedor el ocaso
por charro o indigente que sea,
pero más conmovedor todavía
es aquel brillo desesperado y final
que herrumbra la llanura
cuando en el horizonte nada recuerda
la vanagloria del poniente.
Nos duele sostener esa luz tirante y distinta,
que es una alucinación que impone al espacio
el unánime miedo de la sombra
y que cesa de golpe
cuando notamos su falsía,
como se desbarata un sueño
cuando el soñador advierte que duerme.

AFTERGLOW

Sunset is always disturbing
whether theatrical or muted,
but still more disturbing
is that last desperate glow
that turns the plain to rust
when on the horizon nothing is left
of the pomp and clamor of the setting sun.
How hard holding on to that light, so tautly drawn
    and different,
that hallucination which the human fear of the dark
imposes on space
and which ceases at once
the moment we realize its falsity,
the way a dream is broken
the moment the sleeper knows he is dreaming.

                    [*Norman Thomas di Giovanni*]

AMANECER

En la honda noche universal
que apenas contradicen los macilentos faroles
una racha perdida
ha ofendido las calles taciturnas
como presentimiento tembloroso
del amanecer horrible que ronda
igual que una mentira
los arrabales desmantelados del mundo.
Curioso de la descansada tiniebla
y acobardado por la amenaza del alba
resentí la tremenda conjetura
de Schopenhauer y de Berkeley
que declara que el mundo
es una actividad de la mente,
un sueño de las almas,
sin base ni propósito ni volumen.
Y ya que las ideas
no son eternas como el mármol
sino inmortales como una selva o un río,
la especulación anterior
asumió otra forma en el alba
y la superstición de esa hora
cuando la luz como una enredadera
va a implicar las paredes de la sombra,
doblegó mi razón
y trazó el capricho siguiente:
Si están ajenas de sustancia las cosas
y si esta numerosa Buenos Aires
equiparable en complicación a un ejército,
no es más que un sueño
que logran en compartida magia las almas,
hay un instante
en que peligra desaforadamente su ser
y es el instante estremecido del alba,
cuando son pocos los que sueñan el mundo

DAYBREAK

In the deep universal night
scarcely dispelled by the flickering gaslamps
a gust of wind coming out of nowhere
stirs the silent streets
with a trembling presentiment
of the hideous dawn that haunts
like some lie
the tumbledown outskirts of cities all over the world.
Under the spell of the refreshing darkness
and intimidated by the threat of dawn,
I felt again that tremendous conjecture
of Schopenhauer and Berkeley
which declares the world
an activity of the mind,
a dream of souls,
without foundation or purpose or volume.
And since ideas
are not like marble, everlasting,
but ever-renewing like a forest or a river,
the previous speculation
took another form in the dawn,
and the superstition of the hour,
when the light like a vine
begins twining itself to walls still in shadow,
dominated my reason
and projected the following whim:
If all things are devoid of matter
and if this populous Buenos Aires
comparable to an army in complexity
is no more than a dream
arrived at in magic by souls working together,
there's a moment
in which the city's existence is at the brink of danger
      and disorder
and that is the trembling moment of dawn

y sólo algunos trasnochadores conservan
cenicienta y apenas bosquejada
la visión de las calles
que definirán después con los otros.
¡Hora en que el sueño pertinaz de la vida
está en peligro de quebranto,
hora en que le sería fácil a Dios
matar del todo su obra!

Pero otra vez el mundo se ha salvado.
La luz discurre inventando sucios colores
y con algún remordimiento
de mi complicidad en la resurrección cotidiana
solicito mi casa,
atónita y glacial en la luz blanca,
mientras un pájaro detiene el silencio
y la noche gastada
se ha quedado en los ojos de los ciegos.

when those who are dreaming the world are few
and only a handful of night owls preserve
ashen and sketchy
a vision of the streets
which they will afterward define for others.
The hour in which the persistent dream of life
is in danger of breaking down,
the hour in which God might easily
destroy all his work!

But once more the world comes to its own rescue.
The light streaks in inventing dirty colors
and with a tremor of remorse
for my complicity in the daily rebirth
I seek my house,
amazed and icelike in the white glare,
while a songbird holds the silence back
and the spent night
lives on in the eyes of the blind.

[*Norman Thomas di Giovanni*]

CARNICERIA

Más vil que un lupanar
la carnicería rubrica como una afrenta la calle.
Sobre el dintel
una ciega cabeza de vaca
preside el aquelarre
de carne charra y mármoles finales
con la remota majestad de un ídolo.

AT THE BUTCHER'S

Meaner than a house of prostitution
the meat market flaunts itself in the street like an
    insult.
Above the door
the head of a steer in a blind-eyed stare
watches over the witches' Sabbath
of flayed flesh and marble slabs
with the aloof majesty of an idol.

[*Norman Thomas di Giovanni*]

LLANEZA

A Haydée Lange

Se abre la verja del jardín
con la docilidad de la página
que una frecuente devoción interroga
y adentro las miradas
no precisan fijarse en los objetos
que ya están cabalmente en la memoria.
Conozco las costumbres y las almas
y ese dialecto de alusiones
que toda agrupación humana va urdiendo.
No necesito hablar
ni mentir privilegios;
bien me conocen quienes aquí me rodean,
bien saben mis congojas y mi flaqueza.
Eso es alcanzar lo más alto,
lo que tal vez nos dará el Cielo:
no admiraciones ni victorias
sino sencillamente ser admitidos
como parte de una Realidad innegable,
como las piedras y los árboles.

PLAINNESS

To Haydée Lange

The garden's grillwork gate
opens with the ease of a page
in a much-thumbed book,
and, once inside, our eyes
have no need to dwell on objects
already fixed and exact in memory.
Here habits and minds and the private language
all families invent
are everyday things to me.
What necessity is there to speak
or pretend to be someone else?
The whole house knows me,
they're aware of my worries and weakness.
This is the best that can happen—
what Heaven perhaps will grant us:
not to be wondered at or required to succeed
but simply to be let in
as part of an undeniable Reality,
like stones of the road, like trees.

[*Norman Thomas di Giovanni*]

DESPEDIDA

Entre mi amor y yo han de levantarse
trescientas noches como trescientas paredes
y el mar será una magia entre nosotros.

El tiempo arrancará con dura mano
las calles enzarzadas en mi pecho.
No habrá sino recuerdos.
(Oh tardes merecidas por la pena,
noches esperanzadas de mirarte,
campos desalentados, pobre cielo
humillado en la hondura de los charcos
como un ángel caído . . .
Y tu vivir que agracia mis anhelos
y ese barrio dejado y placentero
que hoy en luz de mi amor se resplandece . . .)

Definitiva como una estatua
entristecerá tu ausencia otros campos.

PARTING

Three hundred nights like three hundred walls
must rise between my love and me
and the sea will be a black art between us.

Time with a hard hand will tear out
the streets tangled in my breast.
Nothing will be left but memories.
(O afternoons earned with suffering,
nights hoping for the sight of you,
dejected vacant lots, poor sky
shamed in the bottom of the puddles
like a fallen angel. . . .
And your life that graces my desire
and that run-down and lighthearted neighborhood
shining today in the glow of my love. . . .)

Final as a statue
your absence will sadden other fields.

[*W. S. Merwin*]

MOON ACROSS THE WAY

[LUNA DE ENFRENTE]

1925

AMOROSA ANTICIPACION

Ni la intimidad de tu frente clara como una fiesta
ni la privanza de tu cuerpo, aún misterioso y tácito
    y de niña,
ni la sucesión de tu vida situándose en palabras o
    silencios
serán favor tan misterioso
como mirar tu sueño implicado
en la vigilia de mis brazos.
Virgen milagrosamente otra vez por la virtud
    absolutoria del sueño,
quieta y resplandeciente como una dicha que la
    memoria elige,
me darás esa orilla de tu vida que tú misma no tienes.
Arrojado a quietud,
divisaré esa playa última de tu ser
y te veré por vez primera, quizá,
como Dios ha de verte,
desbaratada la ficción del Tiempo,
sin el amor, sin mí.

ANTICIPATION OF LOVE

Neither the intimacy of your look, your brow fair as
    a feast day,
nor the favor of your body, still mysterious, reserved,
    and childlike,
nor what comes to me of your life, settling in words
    or silence,
will be so mysterious a gift
as the sight of your sleep, enfolded
in the vigil of my arms.
Virgin again, miraculously, by the absolving power of
    sleep,
quiet and luminous like some happy thing recovered
    by memory,
you will give me that shore of your life that you
    yourself do not own.
Cast up into silence
I shall discern that ultimate beach of your being
and see you for the first time, perhaps,
as God must see you—
the fiction of Time destroyed,
free from love, from me.

[*Robert Fitzgerald*]

EL GENERAL QUIROGA VA EN COCHE
AL MUERE

El madrejón desnudo ya sin una sed de agua
y una luna perdida en el frío del alba
y el campo muerto de hambre, pobre como una
    araña.

El coche se hamacaba rezongando la altura;
un galerón enfático, enorme, funerario.
Cuatro tapaos con pinta de muerte en la negrura
tironeaban seis miedos y un valor desvelado.

Junto a los postillones jineteaba un moreno.
Ir en coche a la muerte ¡qué cosa más oronda!
El general Quiroga quiso entrar en la sombra
llevando seis o siete degollados de escolta.

Esa cordobesada bochinchera y ladina
(meditaba Quiroga) ¿qué ha de poder con mi alma?
Aquí estoy afianzado y metido en la vida
como la estaca pampa bien metida en la pampa.

Yo, que he sobrevivido a millares de tardes
y cuyo nombre pone retemblor en las lanzas,
no he de soltar la vida por estos pedregales.
¿Muere acaso el pampero, se mueren las espadas?

Pero al brillar el día sobre Barranca Yaco
hierros que no perdonan arreciaron sobre él;
la muerte, que es de todos, arreó con el riojano
y una de puñaladas lo mentó a Juan Manuel.

Ya muerto, ya de pie, ya inmortal, ya fantasma,
se presentó al infierno que Dios le había marcado,
y a sus órdenes iban, rotas y desangradas,
las ánimas en pena de hombres y de caballos.

GENERAL QUIROGA RIDES TO HIS DEATH IN A CARRIAGE

The watercourse dry of puddles, not a drop of water left,
and a moon gone out in the cold shiver of the dawn,
and the countryside, poor as a church mouse, dying of hunger.

The coach swayed from side to side, creaking up the slope;
a great bulk of a coach, voluminous, funereal.
Four black horses with a tinge of death in their dark coats
were drawing six souls in terror and one wide awake and bold.

Alongside the postilions a black man was galloping.
To ride to your death in a carriage—what a splendid thing to do!
General Quiroga had in mind to approach the haunts of death
taking six or seven companions with slit throats as escort.

That gang from Córdoba, troublemakers, loud-mouthed, shifty,
(Quiroga was pondering), now what can they possibly do to me?
Here I am strong, secure, well set up in life
like the stake for tethering beasts to, driven deep in the pampa.

I, who have endured through thousands of afternoons
and whose name alone is enough to set the lances quivering,
will not lay down my life in this godforsaken wilderness.
Do the winds from the southwest die, by any chance? Do swords?

But when the brightness of day shone on Barranca Yaco
weapons without mercy swooped in a rage upon him;
death, which is for all, rounded up the man from La Rioja
and more than one thrust of the dagger invoked Juan Manuel de
    Rosas.

Now dead, now on his feet, now immortal, now a ghost,
he reported to the Hell marked out for him by God,
and under his command there marched, broken and bloodless,
the souls in purgatory of his soldiers and his horses.

[*Alastair Reid*]

MANUSCRITO HALLADO EN UN LIBRO DE JOSEPH CONRAD

En las trémulas tierras que exhalan el verano,
El día es invisible de puro blanco. El día
Es una estría cruel en una celosía,
Un fulgor en las costas y una fiebre en el llano.

Pero la antigua noche es honda como un jarro
De agua cóncava. El agua se abre a infinitas huellas,
Y en ociosas canoas, de cara a las estrellas,
El hombre mide el vago tiempo con el cigarro.

El humo desdibuja gris las constelaciones
Remotas. Lo inmediato pierde prehistoria y nombre.
El mundo es unas cuantas tiernas imprecisiones.
El río, el primer río. El hombre, el primer hombre.

MANUSCRIPT FOUND IN
A BOOK OF JOSEPH CONRAD

In the shimmering countries that exude the summer,
The day is blanched in white light. The day
Is a harsh slit across the window shutter,
Dazzle along the coast, and on the plain, fever.

But the ancient night is bottomless, like a jar
Of brimming water. The water reveals limitless wakes,
And in drifting canoes, face inclined to the stars,
Man marks the limp time with a cigar.

The smoke blurs gray across the constellations
Afar. The present sheds past, name, and plan.
The world is a few vague tepid observations.
The river is the original river. Man, the first man.

[*Alastair Reid*]

DULCIA LINQUIMUS ARVA

Una amistad hicieron mis abuelos
con esta lejanía
y conquistaron la intimidad de los campos
y ligaron a su baquía
la tierra, el fuego, el aire, el agua.
Fueron soldados y estancieros
y apacentaron el corazón con mañanas
y el horizonte igual que una bordona
sonó en la hondura de su austera jornada.
Su jornada fue clara como un río
y era fresca su tarde como el agua
oculta del aljibe
y las cuatro estaciones fueron para ellos
como los cuatro versos de la copla esperada.
Descifraron lejanas polvaredas
en carretas o en caballadas
y los alegró el resplandor
con que aviva el sereno la espadaña.
Uno peleó contra los godos,
otro en el Paraguay cansó su espada;
todos supieron del abrazo del mundo
y fue mujer sumisa a su querer la campaña.
Altos eran sus días
hechos de cielo y llano.
Sabiduría de campo afuera la suya,
la de aquel que está firme en el caballo
y que rige a los hombres de la llanura
y los trabajos y los días
y las generaciones de los toros.
Soy un pueblero y ya no sé de esas cosas,
soy hombre de ciudad, de barrio, de calle:
los tranvías lejanos me ayudan la tristeza
con esa queja larga que sueltan en las tardes.

DULCIA LINQUIMUS ARVA

My ancestors struck up a friendship
with these distances
conquering the prairie's closeness,
and to their skill in country ways
linked earth and fire and air and water.
Soldiers and ranchers,
they fed their hearts on mornings,
and the horizon, as if giving back a deep note,
sounded to the depths of their hard work and
    plain days.
The course of their long day's work ran clear
    as a stream,
their evenings were cool as the water
hidden in the patio well,
and to them the four seasons
were like the lines of an expected refrain.
In distant clouds of dust their eyes made out
oxcarts or mustang herds,
and the splendor of the evening dew
glittering on the cattails
could bring them cheer.
One fought the Spaniards,
another exhausted his sword in Paraguay;
they all felt the hold of the world,
and the country was a woman that fell to their love.
Made of sky and plain,
their days were broad and high.
Wisdom of wide-open spaces was theirs,
wisdom of the man who sits firm in the saddle
and oversees plainsmen
and their works and days
and the breeding of cattle.
As a town dweller I no longer know these things.
I come from a city, a neighborhood, a street:
distant streetcars enforce my nostalgia
with the wail they let loose in the night.

[*Norman Thomas di Giovanni*]

CASAS COMO ANGELES

Donde San Juan y Chacabuco se cruzan
vi las casas azules,
vi las casas que tienen colores de aventura.
Eran como banderas
y hondas como el naciente que suelta las afueras.
Las hay color de aurora y las hay color de alba;
su resplandor es una pasión ante la ochava
de la esquina cualquiera, turbia y desanimada.
Yo pienso en las mujeres
que buscarán el cielo de sus patios fervientes.
Pienso en los claros brazos que ilustrarán la tarde
y en el negror de trenzas: pienso en la dicha grave
de mirarse en sus ojos hondos, como parrales.
Empujaré la puerta cancel que es hierro y patio
y habrá una clara niña, ya mi novia, en la sala,
y los dos callaremos, trémulos como llamas,
y la dicha presente se aquietará en pasada.

HOUSES LIKE ANGELS

Where San Juan and Chacabuco intersect
I saw the blue houses,
the houses that wear colors of adventure.
They were like banners
and deep as the dawn that frees the outlying quarters.
Some are daybreak color and some dawn color;
their cool radiance is a passion before the oblique
face of any drab, discouraged corner.
I think of the women
who will be looking skyward from their burning
  dooryards.
I think of the pale arms that make evening glimmer
and of the blackness of braids: I think of the grave
  delight
of being mirrored in their deep eyes, like arbors
  of night.
I will push the gate of iron entering the dooryard
and there will be a fair girl, already mine, in the room.
And the two of us will hush, trembling like flames,
and the present joy will grow quiet in that passed.

[*Robert Fitzgerald*]

MI VIDA ENTERA

Aquí otra vez, los labios memorables, único y
  semejante a vosotros.
Soy esa torpe intensidad que es un alma.
He persistido en la aproximación de la dicha y
  en la privanza del pesar.
He atravesado el mar.
He conocido muchas tierras; he visto una mujer
  y dos o tres hombres.
He querido a una niña altiva y blanca y de una
  hispánica quietud.
He visto un arrabal infinito donde se cumple una
  insaciada inmortalidad de ponientes.
He paladeado numerosas palabras.
Creo profundamente que eso es todo y que ni veré
  ni ejecutaré cosas nuevas.
Creo que mis jornadas y mis noches se igualan en
  pobreza y en riqueza a las de Dios y a las
  de todos los hombres.

MY WHOLE LIFE

Here once again the memorable lips, unique and like yours.
I am this groping intensity that is a soul.
I have got near to happiness and have stood in the shadow
    of suffering.
I have crossed the sea.
I have known many lands; I have seen one woman and two
    or three men.
I have loved a girl who was fair and proud, with a Spanish
    quietness.
I have seen the city's edge, an endless sprawl where the sun
    goes down tirelessly, over and over.
I have relished many words.
I believe deeply that this is all and that I will neither see
    nor accomplish new things.
I believe that my days and my nights, in their poverty and
    their riches, are the equal of God's and of all men's.

[*W. S. Merwin*]

ULTIMO SOL EN VILLA ORTUZAR

Tarde como de Juicio Final.
La calle es una herida abierta en el cielo.
Yo no sé si fue un Angel o un ocaso la claridad
    que ardió en la hondura.
Insistente, como una pesadilla, carga sobre mí la
    distancia.
Al horizonte un alambrado le duele.
El mundo está como inservible y tirado.
En el cielo es de día, pero la noche es traicionera
    en las zanjas.
Toda la luz está en las tapias azules y en ese
    alboroto de chicas.
Ya no sé si es un árbol o es un dios, ese que
    asoma por la verja herrumbrada.
Cuántos países a la vez: el campo, el cielo, las
    afueras.
Hoy he sido rico de calles y de ocaso filoso y de
    la tarde hecha estupor.
Lejos, me devolveré a mi pobreza.

SUNSET OVER VILLA ORTUZAR

Evening like Doomsday.
The street's end opens like a wound on the sky.
Was the brightness burning far away a sunset or an
    angel?
Relentless, like a nightmare, the distance weighs
    on me.
The horizon is tormented by a wire fence.
The world is like something useless, thrown away.
It is still day in the sky, but night is lurking
    in the gullies.
All that is left of the light is in the blue-washed walls
    and in that flock of girls.
Now is it a tree or a god there, showing through
    the rusted gate?
So many terrains at once: the country, the sky, the
    threadbare outskirts.
There were treasures today: streets, whetted sunset,
    the daze of evening.
Far from here, I shall sink again to my poverty.

[*W. S. Merwin*]

SAN MARTIN COPYBOOK

[CUADERNO SAN MARTIN]

1929

As to an occasional copy of verses, there are few men who have leisure to read, and are possessed of any music in their souls, who are not capable of versifying on some ten or twelve occasions during their natural lives: at a proper conjunction of the stars. There is no harm in taking advantage of such occasions.

EDWARD FITZGERALD *in a letter to Bernard Barton (1842)*

FUNDACION MITICA DE BUENOS AIRES

¿Y fue por este río de sueñera y de barro
que las proas vinieron a fundarme la patria?
Irían a los tumbos los barquitos pintados
entre los camalotes de la corriente zaina.

Pensando bien la cosa, supondremos que el río
era azulejo entonces como oriundo del cielo
con su estrellita roja para marcar el sitio
en que ayunó Juan Díaz y los indios comieron.

Lo cierto es que mil hombres y otros mil arribaron
por un mar que tenía cinco lunas de anchura
y aun estaba poblado de sirenas y endriagos
y de piedras imanes que enloquecen la brújula.

Prendieron unos ranchos trémulos en la costa,
durmieron extrañados. Dicen que en el Riachuelo,
pero son embelecos fraguados en la Boca.
Fue una manzana entera y en mi barrio: en Palermo.

Una manzana entera pero en mitá del campo
presenciada de auroras y lluvias y suestadas.
La manzana pareja que persiste en mi barrio:
Guatemala, Serrano, Paraguay, Gurruchaga.

Un almacén rosado como revés de naipe
brilló y en la trastienda conversaron un truco;
el almacén rosado floreció en un compadre,
ya patrón de la esquina, ya resentido y duro.

El primer organito salvaba el horizonte
con su achacoso porte, su habanera y su gringo.
El corralón seguro ya opinaba YRIGOYEN,
algún piano mandaba tangos de Saborido.

THE MYTHICAL FOUNDING OF BUENOS AIRES

And was it along this torpid muddy river
that the prows came to found my native city?
The little painted boats must have suffered the steep surf
among the root-clumps of the horse-brown current.

Pondering well, let us suppose that the river
was blue then like an extension of the sky,
with a small red star inset to mark the spot
where Juan Díaz fasted and the Indians dined.

But for sure a thousand men and other thousands
arrived across a sea that was five moons wide,
still infested with mermaids and sea serpents
and magnetic boulders which sent the compass wild.

On the coast they put up a few ramshackle huts
and slept uneasily. This, they claim, in the Riachuelo,
but that is a story dreamed up in the Boca.
It was really a city block in my district—Palermo.

A whole square block, but set down in open country,
attended by dawns and rains and hard southeasters,
identical to that block which still stands in my
    neighborhood:
Guatemala—Serrano—Paraguay—Gurruchaga.

A general store pink as the back of a playing card
shone bright; in the back there was poker talk.
The corner bar flowered into life as a local bully,
already cock of his walk, resentful, tough.

The first barrel organ teetered over the horizon
with its clumsy progress, its *habaneras,* its wop.
The cart-shed wall was unanimous for YRIGOYEN.
Some piano was banging out tangos by Saborido.

Una cigarrería sahumó como una rosa
el desierto. La tarde se había ahondado en ayeres,
los hombres compartieron un pasado ilusorio.
Sólo faltó una cosa: la vereda de enfrente.

A mí se me hace cuento que empezó Buenos Aires:
La juzgo tan eterna como el agua y el aire.

A cigar store perfumed the desert like a rose.
The afternoon had established its yesterdays,
and men took on together an illusory past.
Only one thing was missing—the street had no other
 side.

Hard to believe Buenos Aires had any beginning.
I feel it to be as eternal as air and water.

[*Alastair Reid*]

ISIDORO ACEVEDO

Es verdad que lo ignoro todo sobre él
—salvo los nombres de lugar y las fechas:
fraudes de la palabra—
pero con temerosa piedad he rescatado su último día,
no el que los otros vieron, el suyo,
y quiero distraerme de mi destino para escribirlo.

Adicto a la conversación porteña del truco,
alsinista nacido del buen lado del Arroyo del Medio,
comisario de frutos del país en el mercado antiguo
    del Once,
comisario de la tercera,
se batió cuando Buenos Aires lo quiso
en Cepeda, en Pavón y en la playa de los Corrales.

Pero mi voz no debe asumir sus batallas,
porque él las arrebató a un sueño esencial.

Porque lo mismo que otros hombres escriben versos,
hizo mi abuelo un sueño.

Cuando una congestión pulmonar lo estaba arrasando
y la inventiva fiebre le falseó la cara del día,
congregó los ardientes documentos de su memoria
para fraguar su sueño.

Esto aconteció en una casa de la calle Serrano,
en el verano ardido del novecientos cinco.

Soñó con dos ejércitos
que entraban en la sombra de una batalla;
enumeró los comandos, las banderas, las unidades.

ISIDORO ACEVEDO

The truth is that I know nothing about him
except for place names and dates—
frauds and failings of the word—
and so with a certain mixture of hesitation and compassion
    I have rescued his last day,
not the one that others saw but his own,
and I want to sidestep my own life now to write about his.

Inveterate cardplayer and habitué of Buenos Aires
    backrooms,
born on the right side of the Arroyo del Medio and a
    follower of Alsina,
inspector of native produce in the old Westside markets,
police inspector of the third district,
when his homeland called him up he fought
in the battles at Cepeda and Pavón and the Stockyard flats.

But my words should not take up his battles
when the vision he wrested from them was so much his own.

For in the same way that other men write verse
my grandfather elaborated a dream.

While a lung ailment ate away at him
and hallucinatory fevers distorted the face of the day,
he assembled the burning documents of his memory
for the forging of his dream.

This took place in a house on Serrano Street
during that burnt-out summer of 1905.

His dream was of two armies
entering the shadow of battle;
he enumerated the commands, the colors, the units.

"Ahora están parlamentando los jefes", dijo en voz
    que le oyeron
y quiso incorporarse para verlos.

Hizo leva de pampa:
vio terreno quebrado para que pudiera aferrarse
    la infantería
y llanura resuelta para que el tirón de la caballería
    fuera invencible.

Hizo una leva última,
congregó los miles de rostros que el hombre sabe
    sin saber después de los años:
caras de barba que se estarán desvaneciendo en
    daguerrotipos,
caras que vivieron junto a la suya en el Puente
    Alsina y Cepeda.

Entró a saco en sus días
para esa visionaria patriada que necesitaba su fe,
    no que una flaqueza le impuso;
juntó un ejército de sombras porteñas
para que lo mataran.

Así, en el dormitorio que miraba al jardín,
murió en un sueño por la patria.

En metáfora de viaje me dijeron su muerte; no la creí.
Yo era chico, yo no sabía entonces de muerte, yo era
    inmortal;
yo lo busqué por muchos días por los cuartos sin luz.

"Now the officers are reviewing their battle plans,"
   he said in a voice you could hear,
and in order to see them he tried sitting up.

He seized a stretch of the prairie,
scouting it for broken terrain, where the infantry could
   hold their ground,
and for a flat place so that the cavalry charge could not
   be turned back.

He made a final levy,
rallying the thousands of faces that a man knows without
   really knowing at the end of his years:
bearded faces now growing dim in daguerreotypes,
faces that lived and died next to his own at the battles
   of Puente Alsina and Cepeda.

In the visionary defense of his country that his faith
   hungered for (and not that his fever imposed),
he plundered his days
and rounded up an army of Buenos Aires ghosts
so as to get himself killed in the fighting.

That was how, in a bedroom that looked onto the garden,
he died out of devotion for his city.

It was in the metaphor of a journey that I was told of
   his death, and I did not believe it.
I was a boy, who knew nothing then of dying; I was immortal,
and afterward for days I searched the sunless rooms for him.

                    [*Norman Thomas di Giovanni*]

LA NOCHE QUE EN EL SUR LO VELARON

A Letizia Alvarez de Toledo

Por el deceso de alguien
—misterio cuyo vacante nombre poseo y cuya realidad
    no abarcamos—
hay hasta el alba una casa abierta en el Sur,
una ignorada casa que no estoy destinado a rever,
pero que me espera esta noche
con desvelada luz en las altas horas del sueño,
demacrada de malas noches, distinta,
minuciosa de realidad.

A su vigilia gravitada en muerte camino
por las calles elementales como recuerdos,
por el tiempo abundante de la noche,
sin más oíble vida
que los vagos hombres de barrio junto al apagado
    almacén
y algún silbido solo en el mundo.

Lento el andar, en la posesión de la espera,
llego a la cuadra y a la casa y a la sincera puerta
    que busco
y me reciben hombres obligados a gravedad
que participaron de los años de mis mayores,
y nivelamos destinos en una pieza habilitada que
    mira al patio
—patio que está bajo el poder y en la integridad
    de la noche—
y decimos, porque la realidad es mayor, cosas
    indiferentes
y somos desganados y argentinos en el espejo
y el mate compartido mide horas vanas.

DEATHWATCH ON THE SOUTHSIDE

To Letizia Alvarez de Toledo

By reason of someone's death—
a mystery whose empty name I know and whose reality
    is beyond us—
a house on the Southside stands open until dawn,
unfamiliar to me, and not to be seen again,
but waiting for me this night
with a wakeful light in the deep hours of sleep—
a house wasted away by bad nights and worn sharp
into a fineness of reality.

Toward its weighty deathwatch I make my way
through streets elementary as memories,
through time grown pure in plenitude of night,
with no more life to be heard
than neighborhood loiterers make near a corner store
and a whistler somewhere, lonely in the nightworld.

In my slow walk, in my expectancy,
I reach the block, the house, the plain door I am
    looking for,
where men constrained to gravity receive me,
men who had a part in my elders' years,
and we size up our destinies in a tidied room over-
    looking the yard,
a yard that is under the power and wholeness of night:
and we speak of indifferent things, reality here being
    greater,
and in the mirror we are Argentine, apathetic,
and the shared maté measures out useless hours.

Me conmueven las menudas sabidurías
que en todo fallecimiento de hombre se pierden
—hábito de unos libros, de una llave, de un cuerpo
    entre los otros—
frecuencias irrecuperables que para él
fueron la amistad de este mundo.
Yo sé que todo privilegio, aunque oscuro, es de
    linaje de milagro
y mucho lo es el de participar en esta vigilia,
reunida alrededor de lo que no se sabe: del Muerto,
reunida para incomunicar o guardar su primera
    noche en la muerte.

(El velorio gasta las caras;
los ojos se nos están muriendo en lo alto como Jesús.)

¿Y el muerto, el increíble?
Su realidad está bajo las flores diferentes de él
y su mortal hospitalidad nos dará
un recuerdo más para el tiempo
y sentenciosas calles del Sur para merecerlas despacio
y brisa oscura sobre la frente que vuelve
y la noche que de la mayor congoja nos libra:
la prolijidad de lo real.

I am touched by the frail wisdoms
lost in every man's death—
his habit of books, of a key, of one body
among the others—
irrecoverable rhythms that for him
composed the friendliness of this world.
I know that every privilege, however obscure, is in
    the line of miracles,
and here is a great one: to take part in this vigil,
gathered around a being no one knows—the Dead;
gathered to set him apart or guard him, his first night
    in death.

(Faces grow haggard with watching:
our eyes are dying on the height like Jesus.)

And the dead man, the unbelievable?
His reality remains under the alien reality of flowers,
and his hospitality in death will give us
one memory more for time
and graven streets on the Southside, one by one to be
    savored,
and a dark breeze in my face as I walk home,
and night that frees us from that ordeal by weariness,
the daily round of the real.

[*Robert Fitzgerald*]

MUERTES DE BUENOS AIRES

I. LA CHACARITA

Porque la entraña del cementerio del Sur
fue saciada por la fiebre amarilla hasta decir basta;
porque los conventillos hondos del Sur
mandaron muerte sobre la cara de Buenos Aires
y porque Buenos Aires no pudo mirar esa muerte,
a paladas te abrieron
en la punta perdida del oeste,
detrás de las tormentas de tierra
y del barrial pesado y primitivo que hizo a los
    cuarteadores.
Allí no había más que el mundo
y las costumbres de las estrellas sobre unas chacras,
y el tren salía de un galpón en Bermejo
con los olvidos de la muerte:
muertos de barba derrumbada y ojos en vela,
muertas de carne desalmada y sin magia.

Trapacerías de la muerte—sucia como el nacimiento
    del hombre—
siguen multiplicando tu subsuelo y así reclutas
tu conventillo de ánimas, tu montonera clandestina
    de huesos
que caen al fondo de tu noche enterrada
lo mismo que a la hondura de un mar,
hacia una muerte sin inmortalidad y sin honra.

Una dura vegetación de sobras en pena
hace fuerza contra tus paredones interminables
cuyo sentido es perdición,
y convencido de corruptibilidad el suburbio
apura su caliente vida a tus pies
en calles traspasadas por una llamarada baja de
    barro

DEATHS OF BUENOS AIRES

I. LA CHACARITA

When the Southside's graveyards,
crammed full of yellow fever, cried out of their
    depths: *Enough,*
when the Southside's clustering tenements
spread death on the face of the city
until Buenos Aires could look at the carnage no longer,
shovel by shovel, they opened you up
on the city's verge where the west drops away—
behind dust storms
and a weight of primordial muck left behind for the
    teamsters.
There was only the world
with its habit of stars rising over a handful of farms,
and trains leaving their sheds in Bermejo
with the gone-and-forgotten:
dead eyes of men keeping watch in unshaven dishevelment,
dead girls, despoiled and unbeautiful flesh, without magic.

The frauds of mortality—stained as in childbirth—
still fatten your subsoil; so you muster up souls
for your compounds, for your hidden contingent of bones
dropped into holes or buried away in your night
as if drowned in the depths of a sea,
preparing a death without hope of eternity, without honor.

A hard vegetation, purgatorial rubbish
inured to damnation,
batters your long line of walls
as though nothing were sure but corruption; a slum
hurls its fiery life at your feet
in gutters shot through with a low flame of mud,

[61]

o se aturde con desgano de bandoneones
o con balidos de cornetas sonsas en carnaval.

(El fallo de destino más para siempre,
que dura en mí lo escuché esa noche en tu noche
cuando la guitarra bajo la mano del orillero
dijo lo mismo que las palabras, y ellas decían:
La muerte es vida vivida,
la vida es muerte que viene.)

Mono del cementerio, la Quema
gesticula advenediza muerte a tus pies.
Gastamos y enfermamos la realidad: 210 carros
infaman las mañanas, llevando
a esa necrópolis de humo
las cotidianas cosas que hemos contagiado de
        muerte.

Cúpulas estrafalarias de madera y cruces en alto
se mueven—piezas negras de un ajedrez final—
        por tus calles
y su achacosa majestad va encubriendo
las vergüenzas de nuestras muertes.

En tu disciplinado recinto
la muerte es incolora, hueca, numérica;
se disminuye a fechas y nombres,
muertes de la palabra.

Chacarita:
desaguadero de esta patria de Buenos Aires, cuesta
        final,
barrio que sobrevives a los otros, que sobremueres,
lazareto que estás en esta muerte no en la otra vida,

or stands, dazed and unwilling, in the sound of accordions
or the bleating of carnival horns.

(The destiny given me now, the judgment that nothing
can alter, I heard on that night, in your night,
when the guitar and the words joined under the hands
of the player—one of the dispossessed poor who lives out
   his life
on the fringes—and the two sang as one:
Death is life lived away,
life is death coming on.)

Cremator of all and mimic of graveyards,
La Quema summons that garbage of death to sit at your
   feet, a passing intruder.
We exhaust and infect all reality: 210 cartloads a day
to outrage the mornings, on their way
to this smoking necropolis
with a waste of quotidian things we have fouled with
   mortality.

Funeral coaches with their nondescript cupolas of wood,
   and raised crosses
move through your streets—black pawns on an ultimate
chessboard—whose festering pomp covers over
the shame of our dying.

In the tidy enclaves
of your graveyards, death keeps colorless, void, and
   statistical,
subsides into birth dates and family names,
the dying away of the word.

Chacarita:
sink of a nation, Buenos Aires sloping away to the end,
barrio outliving all others, or outdying them,
pesthouse of our death, not of a life yet to come,

he oído tu palabra de caducidad y no creo en ella,
porque tu misma convicción de tragedia es acto de
vida
y porque la plenitud de una sola rosa es más que
tus mármoles.

II. LA RECOLETA

Aquí es pundonorosa la muerte,
aquí es la recatada muerte porteña,
la consanguínea de la duradera luz venturosa
del atrio del Socorro
y de la ceniza minuciosa de los braseros
y del fino dulce de leche de los cumpleaños
y de las hondas dinastías de patios.
Se acuerdan bien con ella
esas viejas dulzuras y también los viejos rigores.

Tu frente es el pórtico valeroso
y la generosidad de ciego del árbol
y la dicción de pájaros que aluden, sin saberla,
    a la muerte
y el redoble, endiosador de pechos, de los tambores
en los entierros militares;
tu espalda, los tácitos conventillos del Norte
y el paredón de las ejecuciones rosistas.

Crece en disolución bajo los sufragios de mármol
la nación irrepresentable de muertos
que se deshumanizaron en tu tiniebla
desde que María de los Dolores Maciel, niña del
    Uruguay
—simiente de tu jardín para el cielo—
se durmió, tan poca cosa, en tu descampado.

Pero yo quiero demorarme en el pensamiento
de las livianas flores que son tu comentario piadoso

I have heard all your doddering words and believe none
    of them;
your insistence on tragedy is enough to confirm all
    our living,
and one rose in its bounty exceeds all your marble.

II. LA RECOLETA

Death is scrupulous here; here, in this city of ports,
death is circumspect:
a blood-kinship of enduring and provident light
reaching out from the courts of the *Socorro,*
from the ash burnt to bits in the braziers,
to the sugar-and-milk of a holiday treat
and a depth of patios like a dynasty.
Old sweetnesses, old rigors meet
and are one in the graveyards of *La Recoleta.*

At your summit, the portico's bravery,
a tree's blind solicitude,
birds prattling of death without ever suspecting it,
a ruffle of drums from the veterans' burial plot
to hearten the bypasser;
at your shoulder, hidden away, the tenements of the
    Northside,
the walls of the executioner, Rosas.

Here a nation of unrepresentable dead
thrives on decay under a suffrage of marble,
since the day that the earliest seed in your garden,
    destined for heaven,
Uruguay's child,
María de los Dolores Maciel, dropped off to sleep—
the least of your buried—in your waste desolation.

Here something holds me: I think
of the fatuous flowers that speak out so piously now in
    your name—

—suelo amarillo bajo las acacias de tu costado,
flores izadas a conmemoración en tus mausoleos—
y en el porqué de su vivir gracioso y dormido
junto a las terribles reliquias de los que amamos.

Dije el problema y diré también su palabra:
Siempre las flores vigilaron la muerte,
porque siempre los hombres incomprensiblemente
    supimos
que su existir dormido y gracioso
es el que mejor puede acompañar a los que murieron
sin ofenderlos con soberbia de vida,
sin ser más vida que ellos.

the leaf-yellow clay under the fringe of acacia,
memorial wreaths lifted up in your family crypts—
why do they stay here, in their sleepy and delicate way,
side by side with the terrible keepsakes of those whom
      we loved?

I put the hard question and venture an answer:
our flowers keep perpetual watch on the dead
because we all incomprehensibly know
that their sleepy and delicate presence
is all we can offer the dead to take with them in their dying,
without giving offense through the pride of our living
or seeming more alive than the dead.

[Ben Belitt]

A FRANCISCO LOPEZ MERINO

Si te cubriste, por deliberada mano, de muerte,
si tu voluntad fue rehusar todas las mañanas del mundo,
es inútil que palabras rechazadas te soliciten,
predestinadas a imposibilidad y a derrota.

Sólo nos queda entonces
decir el deshonor de las rosas que no supieron
    demorarte,
el oprobio del día que te permitió el balazo y el fin.

¿Qué sabrá oponer nuestra voz
a lo confirmado por la disolución, la lágrima, el
    mármol?
Pero hay ternuras que por ninguna muerte son menos
—las íntimas, indescifrables noticias que nos cuenta
    la música,
la patria que condesciende a higuera y aljibe,
la ardiente gravitación del amor que justifica el alma—
los cargados minutos
por los que se salva el honor de la realidad.

Pienso en ellos y pienso también, amigo escondido,
que tal vez a imagen de la predilección, obramos
    la muerte,
que la supiste de campanas, niña y graciosa,
hermana de tu aplicada letra de colegial,
y que hubieras querido distraerte en ella como en
    un sueño
en el que hay olvido del mundo, pero amistoso,
en donde es bendecidor todo olvido.

TO FRANCISCO LOPEZ MERINO

If, by your own hand, you brought death on yourself,
if it was your wish to reject all the mornings of this world,
these contradictory words summon you now to no purpose,
doomed as they are to impossibility and failure.

Then all that is left us
is to speak of the roses' dishonor that found no way
    of detaining you,
the opprobrious day that gave you the gunshot and the end.

How can our voices
gainsay what dissolution, the tear-drop, the marble
    confirmed for us?
For surely something is left of our tenderness no death
    can diminish—
the indecipherable, intimate news that music confides to us,
a country pared down to its essence: a fig tree and a
    patio well,
the burning gravitation of love to which our souls bear
    witness—
the weighted minutes
by which reality's honor is salvaged again.

I think of them now, my recondite friend, I think that
perhaps we contrive our own deaths with images of our
    choosing,
that you knew it already, full of bells, childlike and graceful,
a sister of your schoolboy's painstaking hand,
that you might even have thought to humor yourself with
    your death, like a dream
that brings forgetfulness of the world, but in a comradely
    way,
where all oblivion blesses us.

Si esto es verdad y si cuando el tiempo nos deja,
nos queda un sedimento de eternidad, un gusto del
    mundo,
entonces es ligera tu muerte,
como los versos en que siempre estás esperándonos,
entonces no profanarán tu tiniebla
estas amistades que invocan.

If that is the sense of it, and if when time leaves us behind
a grain of eternity clings to us, an aftertaste of the world,
then your death weighs more lightly,
light as the verse wherein you still wait for us always,
and the comradeship that calls to you now
no longer profanes your shadow.

[*Ben Belitt*]

THE SELF AND THE OTHER

[EL OTRO, EL MISMO]

TWO ENGLISH POEMS

To Beatriz Bibiloni Webster de Bullrich

I

The useless dawn finds me in a deserted street-
corner; I have outlived the night.
Nights are proud waves: darkblue topheavy
waves laden with all hues of deep spoil, laden
with things unlikely and desirable.
Nights have a habit of mysterious gifts and re-
fusals, of things half given away, half with-
held, of joys with a dark hemisphere. Nights
act that way, I tell you.
The surge, that night, left me the customary
shreds and odd ends: some hated friends to
chat with, music for dreams, and the smoking of bitter ashes. The things my hungry
heart has no use for.
The big wave brought you.
Words, any words, your laughter; and you so
lazily and incessantly beautiful. We talked
and you have forgotten the words.
The shattering dawn finds me in a deserted
street of my city.
Your profile turned away, the sounds that go to
make your name, the lilt of your laughter:
these are the illustrious toys you have left me.
I turn them over in the dawn, I lose them, I
find them; I tell them to the few stray dogs
and to the few stray stars of the dawn.
Your dark rich life . . .
I must get at you, somehow: I put away those
illustrious toys you have left me, I want your
hidden look, your real smile—that lonely,
mocking smile your cool mirror knows.

II

What can I hold you with?

I offer you lean streets, desperate sunsets, the moon of the ragged suburbs.

I offer you the bitterness of a man who has looked long and long at the lonely moon.

I offer you my ancestors, my dead men, the ghosts that living men have honoured in marble: my father's father killed in the frontier of Buenos Aires, two bullets through his lungs, bearded and dead, wrapped by his soldiers in the hide of a cow; my mother's grandfather—just twentyfour—heading a charge of three hundred men in Perú, now ghosts on vanished horses.

I offer you whatever insight my books may hold, whatever manliness or humour my life.

I offer you the loyalty of a man who has never been loyal.

I offer you that kernel of myself that I have saved, somehow—the central heart that deals not in words, traffics not with dreams and is untouched by time, by joy, by adversities.

I offer you the memory of a yellow rose seen at sunset, years before you were born.

I offer you explanations of yourself, theories about yourself, authentic and surprising news of yourself.

I can give you my loneliness, my darkness, the hunger of my heart; I am trying to bribe you with uncertainty, with danger, with defeat.

1934

LA NOCHE CICLICA

A Sylvina Bullrich

Lo supieron los arduos alumnos de Pitágoras:
Los astros y los hombres vuelven cíclicamente;
Los átomos fatales repetirán la urgente
Afrodita de oro, los tebanos, las ágoras.

En edades futuras oprimirá el centauro
Con el casco solípedo el pecho del lapita;
Cuando Roma sea polvo, gemirá en la infinita
Noche de su palacio fétido el minotauro.

Volverá toda noche de insomnio: minuciosa.
La mano que esto escribe renacerá del mismo
Vientre. Férreos ejércitos construirán el abismo.
(David Hume de Edimburgo dijo la misma cosa.)

No sé si volveremos en un ciclo segundo
Como vuelven las cifras de una fracción periódica;
Pero sé que una oscura rotación pitagórica
Noche a noche me deja en un lugar del mundo

Que es de los arrabales. Una esquina remota
Que puede ser del norte, del sur o del oeste,
Pero que tiene siempre una tapia celeste,
Una higuera sombría y una vereda rota.

Ahí está Buenos Aires. El tiempo, que a los hombres
Trae el amor o el oro, a mí apenas me deja
Esta rosa apagada, esta vana madeja
De calles que repiten los pretéritos nombres

De mi sangre: Laprida, Cabrera, Soler, Suárez . . .
Nombres en que retumban (ya secretas) las dianas,
Las repúblicas, los caballos y las mañanas,
Las felices victorias, las muertes militares.

THE CYCLICAL NIGHT

To Sylvina Bullrich

They knew it, the fervent pupils of Pythagoras:
That stars and men revolve in a cycle,
That fateful atoms will bring back the vital
Gold Aphrodite, Thebans, and agoras.

In future epochs the centaur will oppress
With solid uncleft hoof the breast of the Lapith;
When Rome is dust the Minotaur will moan
Once more in the endless dark of its rank palace.

Every sleepless night will come back in minute
Detail. This writing hand will be born from the same
Womb, and bitter armies contrive their doom.
(Edinburgh's David Hume made this very point.)

I do not know if we will recur in a second
Cycle, like numbers in a periodic fraction;
But I know that a vague Pythagorean rotation
Night after night sets me down in the world

On the outskirts of this city. A remote street
Which might be either north or west or south,
But always with a blue-washed wall, the shade
Of a fig tree, and a sidewalk of broken concrete.

This, here, is Buenos Aires. Time, which brings
Either love or money to men, hands on to me
Only this withered rose, this empty tracery
Of streets with names recurring from the past

In my blood: Laprida, Cabrera, Soler, Suárez . . .
Names in which secret bugle calls are sounding,
Invoking republics, cavalry, and mornings,
Joyful victories, men dying in action.

Las plazas agravadas por la noche sin dueño
Son los patios profundos de un árido palacio
Y las calles unánimes que engendran el espacio
Son corredores de vago miedo y de sueño.

Vuelve la noche cóncava que descifró Anaxágoras;
Vuelve a mi carne humana la eternidad constante
Y el recuerdo ¿el proyecto? de un poema incesante:
"Lo supieron los arduos alumnos de Pitágoras . . ."

1940

Squares weighed down by a night in no one's care
Are the vast patios of an empty palace,
And the single-minded streets creating space
Are corridors for sleep and nameless fear.

It returns, the hollow dark of Anaxagoras;
In my human flesh, eternity keeps recurring
And the memory, or plan, of an endless poem beginning:
"They knew it, the fervent pupils of Pythagoras . . ."

[*Alastair Reid*]

POEMA CONJETURAL

El doctor Francisco Laprida, asesinado el día 22 de setiembre de 1829 por los montoneros de Aldao, piensa antes de morir:

Zumban las balas en la tarde última.
Hay viento y hay cenizas en el viento,
se dispersan el día y la batalla
deforme, y la victoria es de los otros.
Vencen los bárbaros, los gauchos vencen.
Yo, que estudié las leyes y los cánones,
yo, Francisco Narciso de Laprida,
cuya voz declaró la independencia
de estas crueles provincias, derrotado,
de sangre y de sudor manchado el rostro,
sin esperanza ni temor, perdido,
huyo hacia el Sur por arrabales últimos.

Como aquel capitán del Purgatorio
que, huyendo a pie y ensangrentando el llano,
fue cegado y tumbado por la muerte
donde un oscuro río pierde el nombre,
así habré de caer. Hoy es el término.
La noche lateral de los pantanos
me acecha y me demora. Oigo los cascos
de mi caliente muerte que me busca
con jinetes, con belfos y con lanzas.

Yo que anhelé ser otro, ser un hombre
de sentencias, de libros, de dictámenes,
a cielo abierto yaceré entre ciénagas;
pero me endiosa el pecho inexplicable
un júbilo secreto. Al fin me encuentro
con mi destino sudamericano.
A esta ruinosa tarde me llevaba
el laberinto múltiple de pasos

CONJECTURAL POEM

*Doctor Francisco Laprida, set upon and
killed the 22nd of September 1829 by a
band of gaucho militia serving under
Aldao, reflects before he dies:*

Bullets whip the air this last afternoon.
A wind is up, blowing full of cinders
as the day and this chaotic battle
straggle to a close. The gauchos have won:
victory is theirs, the barbarians'.
I, Francisco Narciso Laprida,
who studied both canon law and civil
and whose voice declared the independence
of this entire untamed territory,
in defeat, my face marked by blood and sweat,
holding neither hope nor fear, the way lost,
strike out for the South through the back country.

Like that captain in *Purgatorio*
who fleeing on foot left blood on the plain
and was blinded and then trampled by death
where an obscure river loses its name,
so I too will fall. Today is the end.
The night and to right and left the marshes—
in ambush, clogging my steps. I hear the
hooves of my own hot death riding me down
with horsemen, frothing muzzles, and lances.

I who longed to be someone else, to weigh
judgments, to read books, to hand down the law,
will lie in the open out in these swamps;
but a secret joy somehow swells my breast.
I see at last that I am face to face
with my South American destiny.
I was carried to this ruinous hour
by the intricate labyrinth of steps

que mis días tejieron desde un día
de la niñez. Al fin he descubierto
la recóndita clave de mis años,
la suerte de Francisco de Laprida,
la letra que faltaba, la perfecta
forma que supo Dios desde el principio.
En el espejo de esta noche alcanzo
mi insospechado rostro eterno. El círculo
se va a cerrar. Yo aguardo que así sea.

Pisan mis pies la sombra de las lanzas
que me buscan. Las befas de mi muerte,
los jinetes, las crines, los caballos,
se ciernen sobre mí . . . Ya el primer golpe,
ya el duro hierro que me raja el pecho,
el íntimo cuchillo en la garganta.

1943

woven by my days from a day that goes
back to my birth. At last I've discovered
the mysterious key to all my years,
the fate of Francisco de Laprida,
the missing letter, the perfect pattern
that was known to God from the beginning.
In this night's mirror I can comprehend
my unsuspected true face. The circle's
about to close. I wait to let it come.

My feet tread the shadows of the lances
that spar for the kill. The taunts of my death,
the horses, the horsemen, the horses' manes,
tighten the ring around me. . . . Now the first
blow, the lance's hard steel ripping my chest,
and across my throat the intimate knife.

[*Norman Thomas di Giovanni*]

A UN POETA MENOR
DE LA ANTOLOGIA

¿Dónde está la memoria de los días
que fueron tuyos en la tierra, y tejieron
dicha y dolor y fueron para ti el universo?

El río numerable de los años
los ha perdido; eres una palabra en un índice.

Dieron a otros gloria interminable los dioses,
inscripciones y exergos y monumentos y puntuales
    historiadores;
de ti sólo sabemos, oscuro amigo,
que oíste al ruiseñor, una tarde.

Entre los asfodelos de la sombra, tu vana sombra
pensará que los dioses han sido avaros.

Pero los días son una red de triviales miserias,
¿y habrá suerte mejor que ser la ceniza
de que está hecho el olvido?

Sobre otros arrojaron los dioses
la inexorable luz de la gloria, que mira las entrañas
    y enumera las grietas,
de la gloria, que acaba por ajar la rosa que venera;
contigo fueron más piadosos, hermano.

En el éxtasis de un atardecer que no será una noche,
oyes la voz del ruiseñor de Teócrito.

TO A MINOR POET OF THE
GREEK ANTHOLOGY

Where now is the memory
of the days that were yours on earth, and wove
joy with sorrow, and made a universe that was your own?

The river of years has lost them
from its numbered current; you are a word in an index.

To others the gods gave glory that has no end:
inscriptions, names on coins, monuments, conscientious
    historians;
all that we know of you, eclipsed friend,
is that you heard the nightingale one evening.

Among the asphodels of the Shadow, your shade, in its
    vanity,
must consider the gods ungenerous.

But the days are a web of small troubles,
and is there a greater blessing
than to be the ash of which oblivion is made?

Above other heads the gods kindled
the inexorable light of glory, which peers into the
    secret parts and discovers each separate fault;
glory, that at last shrivels the rose it reveres;
they were more considerate with you, brother.

In the rapt evening that will never be night
you listen without end to Theocritus' nightingale.

[*W. S. Merwin*]

[87]

PAGINA PARA RECORDAR AL CORONEL SUAREZ, VENCEDOR EN JUNIN

Qué importan las penurias, el destierro,
la humillación de envejecer, la sombra creciente
del dictador sobre la patria, la casa en el Barrio
    del Alto
que vendieron sus hermanos mientras guerreaba,
    los días inútiles
(los días que uno espera olvidar, los días que uno
    sabe que olvidará),
si tuvo su hora alta, a caballo,
en la visible pampa de Junín como en un escenario
    para el futuro,
como si el anfiteatro de montañas fuera el futuro.

Qué importa el tiempo sucesivo si en él
hubo una plenitud, un éxtasis, una tarde.

Sirvió trece años en las guerras de América. Al fin
la suerte lo llevó al Estado Oriental, a campos del
    Río Negro.
En los atardeceres pensaría
que para él había florecido esa rosa:
la encarnada batalla de Junín, el instante infinito
en que las lanzas se tocaron, la orden que movió
    la batalla,
la derrota inicial, y entre los fragores
(no menos brusca para él que para la tropa)
su voz gritando a los peruanos que arremetieran,
la luz, el ímpetu y la fatalidad de la carga,
el furioso laberinto de los ejércitos,
la batalla de lanzas en la que no retumbó un solo
    tiro,
el *godo* que atravesó con el hierro,
la victoria, la felicidad, la fatiga, un principio de
    sueño,

A PAGE TO COMMEMORATE COLONEL SUAREZ, VICTOR AT JUNIN

What do they matter now, the deprivations,
exile, the ignominies of growing old,
the dictator's shadow spreading across the land, the house
in the Barrio del Alto, which his brothers sold while
    he fought,
the pointless days (days one hopes to forget,
days one knows are forgettable),
when he had at least his burning hour on horseback
on the plateau of Junín, a stage for the future,
as if that mountain stage itself were the future?

What is time's monotony to him, who knew
that fulfillment, that ecstasy, that afternoon?

Thirteen years he served in the Wars of Independence. Then
fate took him to Uruguay, to the banks of the Río Negro.
In the dying afternoons he would think
of his moment which had flowered like a rose—
the crimson battle of Junín, the enduring moment
in which the lances crossed, the order of battle,
defeat at first, and in the uproar
(as astonishing to him as to the army)
his voice urging the Peruvians to the attack,
the thrill, the drive, the decisiveness of the charge,
the seething labyrinth of cavalries,
clash of the lances (not a single shot fired),
the Spaniard he ran through with his spear,
the headiness of victory, the exhaustion, the drowsiness
    descending,

y la gente muriendo entre los pantanos,
y Bolívar pronunciando palabras sin duda históricas
y el sol ya occidental y el recuperado sabor del agua
    y del vino,
y aquel muerto sin cara porque la pisó y borró
    la batalla . . .

Su bisnieto escribe estos versos y una tácita voz
desde lo antiguo de la sangre le llega:
—Qué importa mi batalla de Junín si es una gloriosa
    memoria,
una fecha que se aprende para un examen o un lugar
    en el atlas.
La batalla es eterna y puede prescindir de la pompa
de visibles ejércitos con clarines;
Junín son dos civiles que en una esquina maldicen
    a un tirano,
o un hombre oscuro que se muere en la cárcel.

1953

and the men dying in the marshes,
and Bolívar uttering words earmarked no doubt for history,
and the sun in the west by now, and water and wine
tasted as for the first time, and that dead man
whose face the battle had trampled on and obliterated. . . .

His great-grandson is writing these lines,
and a silent voice comes to him out of the past,
out of the blood:

"What does my battle at Junín matter if it is only
a glorious memory, or a date learned by rote
for an examination, or a place in the atlas?
The battle is everlasting and can do without
the pomp of actual armies and of trumpets.
Junín is two civilians cursing a tyrant
on a street corner,
or an unknown man somewhere, dying in prison."

[*Alastair Reid*]

MATEO, XXV, 30

El primer puente de Constitución y a mis pies
Fragor de trenes que tejían laberintos de hierro.
Humo y silbidos escalaban la noche,
Que de golpe fue el Juicio Universal. Desde el
    invisible horizonte
Y desde el centro de mi ser, una voz infinita
Dijo estas cosas (estas cosas, no estas palabras,
Que son mi pobre traducción temporal de una sola
    palabra):
—Estrellas, pan, bibliotecas orientales y occidentales,
Naipes, tableros de ajedrez, galerías, claraboyas y
    sótanos,
Un cuerpo humano para andar por la tierra,
Uñas que crecen en la noche, en la muerte,
Sombra que olvida, atareados espejos que multiplican,
Declives de la música, la más dócil de las formas
    del tiempo,
Fronteras del Brasil y del Uruguay, caballos y mañanas,
Una pesa de bronce y un ejemplar de la Saga de Grettir,
Algebra y fuego, la carga de Junín en tu sangre,
Días más populosos que Balzac, el olor de la
    madreselva,
Amor y víspera de amor y recuerdos intolerables,
El sueño como un tesoro enterrado, el dadivoso azar
Y la memoria, que el hombre no mira sin vértigo,
Todo eso te fue dado, y también
El antiguo alimento de los héroes:
La falsía, la derrota, la humillación.
En vano te hemos prodigado el océano,
En vano el sol, que vieron los maravillados ojos
    de Whitman;
Has gastado los años y te han gastado,
Y todavía no has escrito el poema.

1953

MATTHEW XXV: 30

The first bridge, Constitution Station. At my feet
The shunting trains trace iron labyrinths.
Steam hisses up and up into the night,
Which becomes at a stroke the night of the Last Judgment.

From the unseen horizon
And from the very center of my being,
An infinite voice pronounced these things—
Things, not words. This is my feeble translation,
Time-bound, of what was a single limitless Word:

"Stars, bread, libraries of East and West,
Playing cards, chessboards, galleries, skylights, cellars,
A human body to walk with on the earth,
Fingernails, growing at nighttime and in death,
Shadows for forgetting, mirrors busily multiplying,
Cascades in music, gentlest of all time's shapes,
Borders of Brazil, Uruguay, horses and mornings,
A bronze weight, a copy of the Grettir Saga,
Algebra and fire, the charge at Junín in your blood,
Days more crowded than Balzac, scent of the honeysuckle,
Love and the imminence of love and intolerable
    remembering,
Dreams like buried treasure, generous luck,
And memory itself, where a glance can make men dizzy—
All this was given to you and with it
The ancient nourishment of heroes—
Treachery, defeat, humiliation.
In vain have oceans been squandered on you, in vain
The sun, wonderfully seen through Whitman's eyes.
You have used up the years and they have used up you,
And still, and still, you have not written the poem."

[*Alastair Reid*]

[93]

EL PUÑAL

A Margarita Bunge

En un cajón hay un puñal.

Fue forjado en Toledo, a fines del siglo pasado;
Luis Melián Lafinur se lo dio a mi padre,
que lo trajo del Uruguay; Evaristo Carriego
lo tuvo alguna vez en la mano.

Quienes lo ven tienen que jugar un rato con
él; se advierte que hace mucho que lo
buscaban; la mano se apresura a apretar la
empuñadura que la espera; la hoja obediente
y poderosa juega con precisión en la vaina.

Otra cosa quiere el puñal.

Es más que una estructura hecha de metales;
los hombres lo pensaron y lo formaron para
un fin muy preciso; es, de un modo eterno,
el puñal que anoche mató a un hombre en
Tacuarembó y los puñales que mataron a
César. Quiere matar, quiere derramar brusca
sangre.

En un cajón del escritorio, entre borradores y
cartas, interminablemente sueña el puñal su
sencillo sueño de tigre, y la mano se anima
cuando lo rige porque el metal se anima,
el metal que presiente en cada contacto
al homicida para quien lo crearon los
hombres.

A veces me da lástima. Tanta dureza, tanta fe,
tan impasible o inocente soberbia, y los
años pasan, inútiles.

THE DAGGER

To Margarita Bunge

A dagger rests in a drawer.

It was forged in Toledo at the end of the last century. Luis Melián Lafinur gave it to my father, who brought it from Uruguay. Evaristo Carriego once held it in his hand.

Whoever lays eyes on it has to pick up the dagger and toy with it, as if he had always been on the lookout for it. The hand is quick to grip the waiting hilt, and the powerful obeying blade slides in and out of the sheath with a click.

This is not what the dagger wants.

It is more than a structure of metal; men conceived it and shaped it with a single end in mind. It is, in some eternal way, the dagger that last night knifed a man in Tacuarembó and the daggers that rained on Caesar. It wants to kill, it wants to shed sudden blood.

In a drawer of my writing table, among draft pages and old letters, the dagger dreams over and over its simple tiger's dream. On wielding it the hand comes alive because the metal comes alive, sensing itself, each time handled, in touch with the killer for whom it was forged.

At times I am sorry for it. Such power and single-mindedness, so impassive or innocent its pride, and the years slip by, unheeding.

[*Norman Thomas di Giovanni*]

UNA BRUJULA

A Esther Zemborain de Torres

Todas las cosas son palabras del
Idioma en que Alguien o Algo, noche y día,
Escribe esa infinita algarabía
Que es la historia del mundo. En su tropel

Pasan Cartago y Roma, yo, tú, él,
Mi vida que no entiendo, esta agonía
De ser enigma, azar, criptografía
Y toda la discordia de Babel.

Detrás del nombre hay lo que no se nombra;
Hoy he sentido gravitar su sombra
En esta aguja azul, lúcida y leve,

Que hacia el confín de un mar tiende su empeño,
Con algo de reloj visto en un sueño
Y algo de ave dormida que se mueve.

COMPASS

To Esther Zemborain de Torres

All things are words of some strange tongue, in thrall
To Someone, Something, who both day and night
Proceeds in endless gibberish to write
The history of the world. In that dark scrawl

Rome is set down, and Carthage, I, you, all,
And this my being which escapes me quite,
My anguished life that's cryptic, recondite,
And garbled as the tongues of Babel's fall.

Beyond the name there lies what has no name;
Today I have felt its shadow stir the aim
Of this blue needle, light and keen, whose sweep

Homes to the utmost of the sea its love,
Suggestive of a watch in dreams, or of
Some bird, perhaps, who shifts a bit in sleep.

[*Richard Wilbur*]

UN POETA DEL SIGLO XIII

Vuelve a mirar los arduos borradores
De aquel primer soneto innominado,
La página arbitraria en que ha mezclado
Tercetos y cuartetos pecadores.

Lima con lenta pluma sus rigores
Y se detiene. Acaso le ha llegado
Del porvenir y de su horror sagrado
Un rumor de remotos ruiseñores.

¿Habrá sentido que no estaba solo
Y que el arcano, el increíble Apolo
Le había revelado un arquetipo,

Un ávido cristal que apresaría
Cuanto la noche cierra o abre el día:
Dédalo, laberinto, enigma, Edipo?

A POET OF THE THIRTEENTH CENTURY

Think of him laboring in the Tuscan halls
On the first sonnet (that word still unsaid),
The undistinguished pages, filled with sad
Triplets and quatrains, without heads or tails.

Slowly he shapes it; yet the impulse fails.
He stops, perhaps at a strange slight music shed
From time coming and its holy dread,
A murmuring of far-off nightingales.

Did he sense that others were to follow,
That the arcane, incredible Apollo
Had revealed an archetypal thing,

A whirlpool mirror that would draw and hold
All that night could hide or day unfold:
Daedalus, labyrinth, riddle, Oedipus King?

[*William Ferguson*]

UN SOLDADO DE URBINA

Sospechándose indigno de otra hazaña
Como aquella en el mar, este soldado,
A sórdidos oficios resignado,
Erraba oscuro por su dura España.

Para borrar o mitigar la saña
De lo real, buscaba lo soñado
Y le dieron un mágico pasado
Los ciclos de Rolando y de Bretaña.

Contemplaría, hundido el sol, el ancho
Campo en que dura un resplandor de cobre;
Se creía acabado, solo y pobre,

Sin saber de qué música era dueño;
Atravesando el fondo de algún sueño,
Por él ya andaban don Quijote y Sancho.

A SOLDIER OF URBINA

Feeling himself unfitted for the strain
Of battles like the last he fought at sea,
This soldier, doomed to sordid usury,
Wandered unknown throughout his own harsh Spain.

To blot out or to mitigate the pain
Of all reality, he hid in dream;
A magic past was opened up to him
Through Roland and the tales of Ancient Britain.

At sunset he would contemplate the vast
Plain with its copper light lingering on;
He felt himself defeated, poor, alone,

Ignorant of what music he was master;
Already, in the still depths of some dream,
Don Quixote and Sancho were alive in him.

[*Alastair Reid*]

LIMITES

De estas calles que ahondan el poniente,
Una habrá (no sé cuál) que he recorrido
Ya por última vez, indiferente
Y sin adivinarlo, sometido

A Quién prefija omnipotentes normas
Y una secreta y rígida medida
A las sombras, los sueños y las formas
Que destejen y tejen esta vida.

Si para todo hay término y hay tasa
Y última vez y nunca más y olvido
¿Quién nos dirá de quién, en esta casa,
Sin saberlo, nos hemos despedido?

Tras el cristal ya gris la noche cesa
Y del alto de libros que una trunca
Sombra dilata por la vaga mesa,
Alguno habrá que no leeremos nunca.

Hay en el Sur más de un portón gastado
Con sus jarrones de mampostería
Y tunas, que a mi paso está vedado
Como si fuera una litografía.

Para siempre cerraste alguna puerta
Y hay un espejo que te aguarda en vano;
La encrucijada te parece abierta
Y la vigila, cuadrifronte, Jano.

Hay, entre todas tus memorias, una
Que se ha perdido irreparablemente;
No te verán bajar a aquella fuente
Ni el blanco sol ni la amarilla luna.

LIMITS

Of all the streets that blur into the sunset,
There must be one (which, I am not sure)
That I by now have walked for the last time
Without guessing it, the pawn of that Someone

Who fixes in advance omnipotent laws,
Sets up a secret and unwavering scale
For all the shadows, dreams, and forms
Woven into the texture of this life.

If there is a limit to all things and a measure
And a last time and nothing more and forgetfulness,
Who will tell us to whom in this house
We without knowing it have said farewell?

Through the dawning window night withdraws
And among the stacked books which throw
Irregular shadows on the dim table,
There must be one which I will never read.

There is in the South more than one worn gate,
With its cement urns and planted cactus,
Which is already forbidden to my entry,
Inaccessible, as in a lithograph.

There is a door you have closed forever
And some mirror is expecting you in vain;
To you the crossroads seem wide open,
Yet watching you, four-faced, is a Janus.

There is among all your memories one
Which has now been lost beyond recall.
You will not be seen going down to that fountain
Neither by white sun nor by yellow moon.

No volverá tu voz a lo que el persa
Dijo en su lengua de aves y de rosas,
Cuando al ocaso, ante la luz dispersa,
Quieras decir inolvidables cosas.

¿Y el incesante Ródano y el lago,
Todo ese ayer sobre el cual hoy me inclino?
Tan perdido estará como Cartago
Que con fuego y con sal borró el latino.

Creo en el alba oír un atareado
Rumor de multitudes que se alejan;
Son lo que me ha querido y olvidado;
Espacio y tiempo y Borges ya me dejan.

You will never recapture what the Persian
Said in his language woven with birds and roses,
When, in the sunset, before the light disperses,
You wish to give words to unforgettable things.

And the steadily flowing Rhone and the lake,
All that vast yesterday over which today I bend?
They will be as lost as Carthage,
Scourged by the Romans with fire and salt.

At dawn I seem to hear the turbulent
Murmur of crowds milling and fading away;
They are all I have been loved by, forgotten by;
Space, time, and Borges now are leaving me.

[*Alastair Reid*]

UN SAJON (A.D. *449*)

Ya se había hundido la encorvada luna;
Lento en el alba el hombre rubio y rudo
Pisó con receloso pie desnudo
La arena minuciosa de la duna.

Más allá de la pálida bahía,
Blancas tierras miró y negros alcores,
En esa hora elemental del día
En que Dios no ha creado los colores.

Era tenaz. Obraron su fortuna
Remos, redes, arado, espada, escudo;
La dura mano que guerreaba pudo
Grabar con hierro una porfiada runa.

De una tierra de ciénagas venía
A esta que roen los pesados mares;
Sobre él se abovedaba como el día
El Destino, y también sobre sus lares,

Woden o Thunor, que con torpe mano
Engalanó de trapos y de clavos
Y en cuyo altar sacrificó inhumano
Caballos, perros, pájaros y esclavos.

Para cantar memorias o alabanzas
Amonedaba laboriosos nombres;
La guerra era el encuentro de los hombres
Y también el encuentro de las lanzas.

Su mundo era de magias en los mares,
De reyes y de lobos y del Hado
Que no perdona y del horror sagrado
Que hay en el corazón de los pinares.

A SAXON (A.D. *449*)

By now it had gone down, the sickle moon;
Slowly in the dawn the man, blond and blunt,
Trod with a tentative bare foot
The fine and shifting sand grains of the dune.

Far off, beyond the pallor of the bay,
His eye took in blank lowlands and dark hills
In that first waking moment of the day
When God has not yet brought to light the colors.

He was dogged. His survival counted on
His oars and nets, his plough, his sword, his shield;
The hand that was hard in battle still was able
To carve with iron point a stubborn rune.

He came from a land of tidal swamp and marsh
To one eroded by relentless seas;
Destiny towered above him like the arch
Of the day, and over his household deities,

Woden or Thunor, whom with clumsy hand
He garlanded with rags and iron nails,
And on whose altar offered up, indifferent,
His animals—horses, dogs, fowls—and slaves.

To give a voice to memories or hymns
He coined laborious names and metaphors;
War was a coming face to face of men,
A crossing of swords, a colloquy of spears.

His world was one of wonders on the seas,
Of kings and wolves and an impervious Fate
Which grants no pardon, and of fearful spells
Lurking in the black heart of the pine wood.

Traía las palabras esenciales
De una lengua que el tiempo exaltaría
A música de Shakespeare: noche, día,
Agua, fuego, colores y metales,

Hambre, sed, amargura, sueño, guerra,
Muerte y los otros hábitos humanos;
En arduos montes y en abiertos llanos,
Sus hijos engendraron a Inglaterra.

He brought with him the elemental words
Of a language that in time would flower
In Shakespeare's harmonies: night, day,
Water, fire, words for metals and colors,

Hunger, thirst, bitterness, sleep, fighting,
Death, and other grave concerns of men;
On broad meadows and in tangled woodland
The sons he bore brought England into being.

[Alastair Reid]

EL GOLEM

Si (como el griego afirma en el Cratilo)
El nombre es arquetipo de la cosa,
En las letras de *rosa* está la rosa
Y todo el Nilo en la palabra *Nilo*.

Y, hecho de consonantes y vocales,
Habrá un terrible Nombre, que la esencia
Cifre de Dios y que la Omnipotencia
Guarde en letras y sílabas cabales.

Adán y las estrellas lo supieron
En el Jardín. La herrumbre del pecado
(Dicen los cabalistas) lo ha borrado
Y las generaciones lo perdieron.

Los artificios y el candor del hombre
No tienen fin. Sabemos que hubo un día
En que el pueblo de Dios buscaba el Nombre
En las vigilias de la judería.

No a la manera de otras que una vaga
Sombra insinúan en la vaga historia,
Aún está verde y viva la memoria
De Judá León, que era rabino en Praga.

Sediento de saber lo que Dios sabe,
Judá León se dio a permutaciones
De letras y a complejas variaciones
Y al fin pronunció el Nombre que es la Clave,

La Puerta, el Eco, el Huésped y el Palacio,
Sobre un muñeco que con torpes manos
Labró, para enseñarle los arcanos
De las Letras, del Tiempo y del Espacio.

THE GOLEM

If every name is (as the Greek maintains
In the *Cratylus*) the archetype of its thing,
Among the letters of *ring*, resides the ring,
And in the word *Nile* all the Nile remains.

Then, made up of vowels and consonants,
Encoding God's essence, should exist some Name
Whose exact syllables and letters frame
Within them, terribly, Omnipotence.

Adam and all the stars had known it, placed
There in the Garden. The corrosive rust
Of sin (cabalists say) has long effaced
The Name that generations since have lost.

Human innocency and human guile
Are boundless: it is known that a day came
When the Chosen People pursued the Name
Over the wakeful ghetto's midnight oil.

Unlike the way of those who, as in fog,
Beam a dim shadow in dim history,
Green and alive remains the memory
Of Judah, the Hohe Rabbi Löw of Prague.

Yearning to know that which the Deity
Knows, the Rabbi turned to permutations
Of letters in complicated variations,
And finally pronounced the Name which is the Key,

The Entry Gate, the Echo, Host, and Mansion,
Over a dummy at which, with sluggish hand,
He labored hard that it might understand
Secrets of Time, Space, Being, and Extension.

El simulacro alzó los soñolientos
Párpados y vio formas y colores
Que no entendió, perdidos en rumores,
Y ensayó temerosos movimientos.

Gradualmente se vio (como nosotros)
Aprisionado en esta red sonora
De Antes, Después, Ayer, Mientras, Ahora,
Derecha, Izquierda, Yo, Tú, Aquellos, Otros.

(El cabalista que ofició de numen
A la vasta criatura apodó Golem;
Estas verdades las refiere Scholem
En un docto lugar de su volumen.)

El rabí le explicaba el universo
(*Esto es mi pie; esto el tuyo; esto la soga*)
Y logró, al cabo de años, que el perverso
Barriera bien o mal la sinagoga.

Tal vez hubo un error en la grafía
O en la articulación del Sacro Nombre;
A pesar de tan alta hechicería,
No aprendió a hablar el aprendiz de hombre.

Sus ojos, menos de hombre que de perro
Y harto menos de perro que de cosa,
Seguían al rabí por la dudosa
Penumbra de las piezas del encierro.

Algo anormal y tosco hubo en el Golem,
Ya que a su paso el gato del rabino
Se escondía. (Ese gato no está en Scholem
Pero, a través del tiempo, lo adivino.)

Elevando a su Dios manos filiales,
Las devociones de su Dios copiaba
O, estúpido y sonriente, se ahuecaba
En cóncavas zalemas orientales.

The simulacrum raised its heavy, lowered
Eyelids and perceived colors and forms;
It understood not; lost in loud alarms,
It started to take groping paces forward.

And like ourselves, it gradually became
Locked in the sonorous meshes of the net
Of After, Before, Tomorrow, Meanwhile, Yet,
Right, Left, You, Me, and Different and Same.

(The cabalist from whom the creature took
Its inspiration called the weird thing Golem—
But all these matters are discussed by Scholem
In a most learned passage in his book.)

The rabbi revealed to it the universe
(*This is my foot; that's yours; this is a log*)
And after years of training, the perverse
Pupil managed to sweep the synagogue.

Perhaps there was a faulty text, or breach
In the articulation of the Name;
The magic was the highest—all the same,
The apprentice person never mastered speech.

Less a man's than a dog's, less a dog's, well,
Even than a thing's, the creature's eyes
Would always turn to follow the rabbi's
Steps through the dubious shadows of his cell.

Something eerie, gross, about the Golem,
For, at his very coming, the rabbi's cat
Would vanish. (The cat cannot be found in Scholem;
Across the years, I divine it, for all that.)

Toward God it would extend those filial palms,
Aping the devotions of its God,
Or bend itself, the stupid, grinning clod,
In hollow, Orientalized salaams.

El rabí lo miraba con ternura
Y con algún horror. *¿Cómo* (se dijo)
Pude engendrar este penoso hijo
Y la inacción dejé, que es la cordura?

¿Por qué di en agregar a la infinita
Serie un símbolo más? ¿Por qué a la vana
Madeja que en lo eterno se devana,
Di otra causa, otro efecto y otra cuita?

En la hora de angustia y de luz vaga,
En su Golem los ojos detenía.
¿Quién nos dirá las cosas que sentía
Dios, al mirar a su rabino en Praga?

1958

The rabbi gazed on it with tender eyes
And terror. *How* (he asked) *could it be done*
That I engender this distressing son?
Inaction is wisdom. I left off being wise.

To an infinite series why was it for me
To add another integer? To the vain
Hank that is spun out in Eternity
Another cause or effect, another pain?

At the anguished hour when the light gets vague
Upon his Golem his eyes would come to rest.
Who can tell us the feelings in His breast
As God gazed on His rabbi there in Prague?

[*John Hollander*]

POEMA DE LOS DONES

A María Esther Vázquez

Nadie rebaje a lágrima o reproche
Esta declaración de la maestría
De Dios, que con magnífica ironía
Me dio a la vez los libros y la noche.

De esta ciudad de libros hizo dueños
A unos ojos sin luz, que sólo pueden
Leer en las bibliotecas de los sueños
Los insensatos párrafos que ceden

Las albas a su afán. En vano el día
Les prodiga sus libros infinitos,
Arduos como los arduos manuscritos
Que perecieron en Alejandría.

De hambre y de sed (narra una historia griega)
Muere un rey entre fuentes y jardines;
Yo fatigo sin rumbo los confines
De esta alta y honda biblioteca ciega.

Enciclopedias, atlas, el Oriente
Y el Occidente, siglos, dinastías,
Símbolos, cosmos y cosmogonías
Brindan los muros, pero inútilmente.

Lento en mi sombra, la penumbra hueca
Exploro con el báculo indeciso,
Yo, que me figuraba el Paraíso
Bajo la especie de una biblioteca.

Algo, que ciertamente no se nombra
Con la palabra *azar,* rige estas cosas;

POEM OF THE GIFTS

To María Esther Vázquez

Let no one impute to self-pity or censure
The power of the thing I affirm: that God
With magnificent irony has dealt me the gift
Of these books and the dark, with one stroke.

He has lifted these eyes, now made lightless,
To be lords of this city of books, though all that they
    read
In my dream of a library are insensible paragraphs
Disclosed to their longing

Each passing day. Vainly dawn multiplies book
After book to infinity, each one
Inaccessible, each lost to me now, like the manuscripts
Alexandria fed to the flame.

Greek anecdote tells of a king who lived among
Gardens and fountains, and died of thirst and starvation;
I toil in the breadth and the depth and the blindness
Of libraries, without strength or direction.

Encyclopedias, atlases, Orient,
Occident, dynasties, ages,
Symbols and cosmos, cosmogonies
Call to me from the walls—ineffectual images!

Painfully probing the dark, I grope toward
The void of the twilight with the point of my faltering
Cane—I for whom Paradise was always a metaphor,
An image of libraries.

Something—no need to prattle of chance
Or contingency—presides over these matters;

Otro ya recibió en otras borrosas
Tardes los muchos libros y la sombra.

Al errar por las lentas galerías
Suelo sentir con vago horror sagrado
Que soy el otro, el muerto, que habrá dado
Los mismos pasos en los mismos días.

¿Cuál de los dos escribe este poema
De un yo plural y de una sola sombra?
¿Qué importa la palabra que me nombra
Si es indiviso y uno el anatema?

Groussac o Borges, miro este querido
Mundo que se deforma y que se apaga
En una pálida ceniza vaga
Que se parece al sueño y al olvido.

Long before me, some other man took these books and the
  dark
In a fading of dusk for his lot.

Astray in meandering galleries,
It comes to me now with a holy, impalpable
Dread, that I am that other, the dead man, and walk
With identical steps and identical days to the end.

Which of us two is writing this poem
In the I of the first person plural, in identical darkness?
What good is the word that speaks for me now in my name,
If the curse of the dark is implacably one and the same?

Groussac or Borges, I watch the delectable
World first disfigure then extinguish itself
In a pallor of ashes, until all that is gone
Seems at one with sleep and at one with oblivion.

                                                    [*Ben Belitt*]

AJEDREZ

I

En su grave rincón, los jugadores
Rigen las lentas piezas. El tablero
Los demora hasta el alba en su severo
Ambito en que se odian dos colores.

Adentro irradian mágicos rigores
Las formas: torre homérica, ligero
Caballo, armada reina, rey postrero,
Oblicuo alfil y peones agresores.

Cuando los jugadores se hayan ido,
Cuando el tiempo los haya consumido,
Ciertamente no habrá cesado el rito.

En el Oriente se encendió esta guerra
Cuyo anfiteatro es hoy toda la tierra.
Como el otro, este juego es infinito.

II

Tenue rey, sesgo alfil, encarnizada
Reina, torre directa y peón ladino
Sobre lo negro y blanco del camino
Buscan y libran su batalla armada.

No saben que la mano señalada
Del jugador gobierna su destino,
No saben que un rigor adamantino
Sujeta su albedrío y su jornada.

También el jugador es prisionero
(La sentencia es de Omar) de otro tablero
De negras noches y de blancos días.

CHESS

I

Set in their studious corners, the players
Move the gradual pieces. Until dawn
The chessboard keeps them in its strict confinement
With its two colors set at daggers drawn.

Within the game itself the forms give off
Their magic rules: Homeric castle, knight
Swift to attack, queen warlike, king decisive,
Slanted bishop, and attacking pawns.

Eventually, when the players have withdrawn,
When time itself has finally consumed them,
The ritual certainly will not be done.

It was in the East this war took fire.
Today the whole earth is its theater.
Like the game of love, this game goes on forever.

II

Faint-hearted king, sly bishop, ruthless queen,
Straightforward castle, and deceitful pawn—
Over the checkered black and white terrain
They seek out and begin their armed campaign.

They do not know it is the player's hand
That dominates and guides their destiny.
They do not know an adamantine fate
Controls their will and lays the battle plan.

The player too is captive of caprice
(The words are Omar's) on another ground
Where black nights alternate with whiter days.

Dios mueve al jugador, y éste, la pieza.
¿Qué dios detrás de Dios la trama empieza
De polvo y tiempo y sueño y agonías?

God moves the player, he in turn the piece.
But what god beyond God begins the round
Of dust and time and sleep and agonies?

[*Alastair Reid*]

ELVIRA DE ALVEAR

Todas las cosas tuvo y lentamente
Todas la abandonaron. La hemos visto
Armada de belleza. La mañana
Y el arduo mediodía le mostraron,
Desde su cumbre, los hermosos reinos
De la tierra. La tarde fue borrándolos.
El favor de los astros (la infinita
Y ubicua red de causas) le había dado
La fortuna, que anula las distancias
Como el tapiz del árabe, y confunde
Deseo y posesión, y el don del verso,
Que transforma las penas verdaderas
En una música, un rumor y un símbolo,
Y el fervor, y en la sangre la batalla
De Ituzaingó y el peso de laureles,
Y el goce de perderse en el errante
Río del tiempo (río y laberinto)
Y en los lentos colores de las tardes.
Todas las cosas la dejaron, menos
Una. La generosa cortesía
La acompañó hasta el fin de su jornada,
Más allá del delirio y del eclipse,
De un modo casi angélico. De Elvira
Lo primero que vi, hace tantos años,
Fue la sonrisa y es también lo último.

ELVIRA DE ALVEAR

She once had everything but one by one
Each thing abandoned her. We saw her armed
With beauty. The morning and the hard light
Of noon from their pinnacle revealed to her
The glorious kingdoms of the world. Evening
Wiped them away. The luck of the stars
(The endless, everpresent web of causes)
Had granted her wealth, which shrinks distances
Like a magic carpet and confuses
Desire and possession; and the gift of verse,
Which works to change real suffering into
Music and to sound and to symbol;
And energy; and in her blood the battle
Of Ituzaingó and the weight of laurels;
And the pleasure of losing oneself in time's
Meandering river (river and maze)
And the evening's slowly shifting colors.
Each thing deserted her, except for one.
Warmhearted graciousness was at her side
Until her final days, beyond her madness
And decline, in an almost angelic way.
Of Elvira what I saw first, years and years
Past, was her smile and it is now the last.

[*Norman Thomas di Giovanni*]

SUSANA SOCA

Con lento amor miraba los dispersos
Colores de la tarde. Le placía
Perderse en la compleja melodía
O en la curiosa vida de los versos.
No el rojo elemental sino los grises
Hilaron su destino delicado,
Hecho a discriminar y ejercitado
En la vacilación y en los matices.
Sin atreverse a hollar este perplejo
Laberinto, miraba desde afuera
Las formas, el tumulto y la carrera,
Como aquella otra dama del espejo.
Dioses que moran más allá del ruego
La abandonaron a ese tigre, el Fuego.

SUSANA SOCA

With gradual love she watched the evening
Colors disperse. How much she enjoyed
Dissolving in the intricate tune
Or in the curious life of verses!
No primal red, but grey upon gray
Embroidered her fastidious fate,
One inured to choosing and practiced
In vacillation, mélange, nuance.
Not daring to enter this doubtful
Labyrinth, she observed (from outside)
The forms, the factions, and the fray,
Like that other lady of the mirror.
The gods who live past all imploring
Abandoned her to that tiger, Fire.

[*Richard Howard and César Rennert*]

EL OTRO TIGRE

And the craft that createth a semblance
MORRIS: *Sigurd the Volsung* (*1876*)

Pienso en un tigre. La penumbra exalta
La vasta Biblioteca laboriosa
Y parece alejar los anaqueles;
Fuerte, inocente, ensangrentado y nuevo,
El irá por su selva y su mañana
Y marcará su rastro en la limosa
Margen de un río cuyo nombre ignora
(En su mundo no hay nombres ni pasado
Ni porvenir, sólo un instante cierto)
Y salvará las bárbaras distancias
Y husmeará en el trenzado laberinto
De los olores el olor del alba
Y el olor deleitable del venado;
Entre las rayas del bambú descifro
Sus rayas y presiento la osatura
Bajo la piel espléndida que vibra.
En vano se interponen los convexos
Mares y los desiertos del planeta;
Desde esta casa de un remoto puerto
De América del Sur, te sigo y sueño,
Oh tigre de las márgenes del Ganges.

Cunde la tarde en mi alma y reflexiono
Que el tigre vocativo de mi verso
Es un tigre de símbolos y sombras,
Una serie de tropos literarios
Y de memorias de la enciclopedia
Y no el tigre fatal, la aciaga joya
Que, bajo el sol o la diversa luna,
Va cumpliendo en Sumatra o en Bengala
Su rutina de amor, de ocio y de muerte.
Al tigre de los símbolos he opuesto
El verdadero, el de caliente sangre,

THE OTHER TIGER

And the craft that createth a semblance
MORRIS: *Sigurd the Volsung (1876)*

A tiger comes to mind. The twilight here
Exalts the vast and busy Library
And seems to set the bookshelves back in gloom;
Innocent, ruthless, bloodstained, sleek,
It wanders through its forest and its day
Printing a track along the muddy banks
Of sluggish streams whose names it does not know
(In its world there are no names or past
Or time to come, only the vivid now)
And makes its way across wild distances
Sniffing the braided labyrinth of smells
And in the wind picking the smell of dawn
And tantalizing scent of grazing deer;
Among the bamboo's slanting stripes I glimpse
The tiger's stripes and sense the bony frame
Under the splendid, quivering cover of skin.
Curving oceans and the planet's wastes keep us
Apart in vain; from here in a house far off
In South America I dream of you,
Track you, O tiger of the Ganges' banks.

It strikes me now as evening fills my soul
That the tiger addressed in my poem
Is a shadowy beast, a tiger of symbols
And scraps picked up at random out of books,
A string of labored tropes that have no life,
And not the fated tiger, the deadly jewel
That under sun or stars or changing moon
Goes on in Bengal or Sumatra fulfilling
Its rounds of love and indolence and death.
To the tiger of symbols I hold opposed
The one that's real, the one whose blood runs hot

El que diezma la tribu de los búfalos
Y hoy, 3 de agosto del 59,
Alarga en la pradera una pausada
Sombra, pero ya el hecho de nombrarlo
Y de conjeturar su circunstancia
Lo hace ficción del arte y no criatura
Viviente de las que andan por la tierra.

Un tercer tigre buscaremos. Este
Será como los otros una forma
De mi sueño, un sistema de palabras
Humanas y no el tigre vertebrado
Que, más allá de las mitologías,
Pisa la tierra. Bien lo sé, pero algo
Me impone esta aventura indefinida,
Insensata y antigua, y persevero
En buscar por el tiempo de la tarde
El otro tigre, el que no está en el verso.

As it cuts down a herd of buffaloes,
And that today, this August third, nineteen
Fifty-nine, throws its shadow on the grass;
But by the act of giving it a name,
By trying to fix the limits of its world,
It becomes a fiction, not a living beast,
Not a tiger out roaming the wilds of earth.

We'll hunt for a third tiger now, but like
The others this one too will be a form
Of what I dream, a structure of words, and not
The flesh and bone tiger that beyond all myths
Paces the earth. I know these things quite well,
Yet nonetheless some force keeps driving me
In this vague, unreasonable, and ancient quest,
And I go on pursuing through the hours
Another tiger, the beast not found in verse.

[*Norman Thomas di Giovanni*]

ALUSION A UNA SOMBRA DE MIL OCHOCIENTOS NOVENTA Y TANTOS

Nada. Sólo el cuchillo de Muraña.
Sólo en la tarde gris la historia trunca.
No sé por qué en las tardes me acompaña
Este asesino que no he visto nunca.
Palermo era más bajo. El amarillo
Paredón de la cárcel dominaba
Arrabal y barrial. Por esa brava
Región anduvo el sórdido cuchillo.
El cuchillo. La cara se ha borrado
Y de aquel mercenario cuyo austero
Oficio era el coraje, no ha quedado
Más que una sombra y un fulgor de acero.
Que el tiempo, que los mármoles empaña,
Salve este firme nombre: Juan Muraña.

ALLUSION TO A SHADOW
OF THE NINETIES

Nothing. Only Muraña's knife.
Only half a tale by gray light.
Who knows why, now it is evening,
This killer I have never seen
Follows me? Palermo was then
A slum beneath the prison wall,
And in those barrens roamed a vile
Knife. His knife. The face has faded
Of that mercenary whose grim
Profession was courage; nothing
Remains but a shadow, a flash
Of steel. Let time, burying marble,
Save one fierce name: Juan Muraña.

[*Richard Howard and César Rennert*]

ALUSION A LA MUERTE DEL CORONEL FRANCISCO BORGES (1833–74)

Lo dejo en el caballo, en esa hora
Crepuscular en que buscó la muerte;
Que de todas las horas de su suerte
Esta perdure, amarga y vencedora.
Avanza por el campo la blancura
Del caballo y del poncho. La paciente
Muerte acecha en los rifles. Tristemente
Francisco Borges va por la llanura.
Esto que lo cercaba, la metralla,
Esto que ve, la pampa desmedida,
Es lo que vio y oyó toda la vida.
Está en lo cotidiano, en la batalla.
Alto lo dejo en su épico universo
Y casi no tocado por el verso.

ALLUSION TO THE DEATH OF COLONEL FRANCISCO BORGES (1833–1874)

I leave him on his horse on that evening
In which he rode across the plain to meet
His death, and of all the hours of his fate
May this one, though bitter, go on living.
White horse, white poncho pick a studied way
Over the flat terrain. Ahead, death lurks
Patiently in the barrels of the guns.
Colonel Borges sadly crosses the plain.
What closed on him, the Remingtons' crackle,
What his eye took in, endless grazing land,
Are what he saw and heard his whole life long.
Here was his home—in the thick of battle.
In his epic world, riding on his horse,
I leave him almost untouched by my verse.

[*Norman Thomas di Giovanni*]

LOS BORGES

Nada o muy poco sé de mis mayores
Portugueses, los Borges: vaga gente
Que prosigue en mi carne, oscuramente,
Sus hábitos, rigores y temores.
Tenues como si nunca hubieran sido
Y ajenos a los trámites del arte,
Indescifrablemente forman parte
Del tiempo, de la tierra y del olvido.
Mejor así. Cumplida la faena,
Son Portugal, son la famosa gente
Que forzó las murallas del Oriente
Y se dio al mar y al otro mar de arena.
Son el rey que en el místico desierto
Se perdió y el que jura que no ha muerto.

THE BORGES

I know little or nothing of the Borges,
My Portuguese forebears. They were a ghostly race,
Who still ply in my body their mysterious
Disciplines, habits, and anxieties.
Shadowy, as if they had never been,
And strangers to the processes of art,
Indecipherably they form a part
Of time, of earth, and of oblivion.
Better so. When everything is said,
They are Portugal, they are that famous people
Who forced the Great Wall of the East, and fell
To the sea, and to that other sea of sand.
They are that king lost on the mystic strand
And those at home who swear he is not dead.

[*Alastair Reid*]

AL INICIAR EL ESTUDIO DE LA
GRAMATICA ANGLOSAJONA

Al cabo de cincuenta generaciones
(Tales abismos nos depara a todos el tiempo)
Vuelvo en la margen ulterior de un gran río
Que no alcanzaron los dragones del viking,
A las ásperas y laboriosas palabras
Que, con una boca hecha polvo,
Usé en los días de Nortumbria y de Mercia,
Antes de ser Haslam o Borges.
El sábado leímos que Julio el César
Fue el primero que vino de Romeburh para develar
    a Bretaña;
Antes que vuelvan los racimos habré escuchado
La voz del ruiseñor del enigma
Y la elegía de los doce guerreros
Que rodean el túmulo de su rey.
Símbolos de otros símbolos, variaciones
Del futuro inglés o alemán me parecen estas palabras
Que alguna vez fueron imágenes
Y que un hombre usó para celebrar el mar o una
    espada;
Mañana volverán a vivir,
Mañana *fyr* no será *fire* sino esa suerte
De dios domesticado y cambiante
Que a nadie le está dado mirar sin un antiguo
    asombro.

Alabado sea el infinito
Laberinto de los efectos y de las causas
Que antes de mostrarme el espejo
En que no veré a nadie o veré a otro
Me concede esta pura contemplación
De un lenguaje del alba.

EMBARKING ON THE STUDY
OF ANGLO-SAXON GRAMMAR

After some fifty generations
(Such gulfs are opened to us all by time)
I come back on the far shore of a vast river
Never reached by the Norsemen's long ships
To the harsh and work-wrought words
Which, with a tongue now dust,
I used in the days of Northumbria and Mercia
Before becoming Haslam or Borges.
Last Saturday we read how Julius Caesar
Was the first who came from Romeburh to seek out Britain;
Before the grapes grow back I shall have listened to
The nightingale of the riddle
And the elegy intoned by the twelve warriors
Round the burial mound of their king.
To me these words seem
Symbols of other symbols, variants
On the English or the German (their descendants),
Yet at some point in time they were fresh images
And a man used them to invoke the sea or a sword.
Tomorrow they will come alive again;
Tomorrow *fyr* will not become *fire* but rather
Some vestige of a changeable tamed god
Whom no one can confront without feeling an ancient fear.

All praise to the inexhaustible
Labyrinth of cause and effect
Which, before unveiling to me the mirror
Where I shall see no one or shall see some other self,
Has granted me this perfect contemplation
Of a language at its dawn.

[*Alastair Reid*]

LUCAS, XXIII

Gentil o hebreo o simplemente un hombre
Cuya cara en el tiempo se ha perdido;
Ya no rescataremos del olvido
Las silenciosas letras de su nombre.

Supo de la clemencia lo que puede
Saber un bandolero que Judea
Clava a una cruz. Del tiempo que antecede
Nada alcanzamos hoy. En su tarea

Ultima de morir crucificado,
Oyó, entre los escarnios de la gente,
Que el que estaba muriéndose a su lado
Era Dios y le dijo ciegamente:

*Acuérdate de mí cuando vinieres
A tu reino,* y la voz inconcebible
Que un día juzgará a todos los seres
Le prometió desde la Cruz terrible

El Paraíso. Nada más dijeron
Hasta que vino el fin, pero la historia
No dejará que muera la memoria
De aquella tarde en que los dos murieron.

Oh amigos, la inocencia de este amigo
De Jesucristo, ese candor que hizo
Que pidiera y ganara el Paraíso
Desde las ignominias del castigo,

Era el que tantas veces al pecado
Lo arrojó y al azar ensangrentado.

LUKE XXIII

Gentile or Jew or simply a man
Whose face has been lost in time,
We shall not save the silent
Letters of his name from oblivion.

What could he know of forgiveness,
A thief whom Judea nailed to a cross?
For us those days are lost.
During his last undertaking,

Death by crucifixion,
He learned from the taunts of the crowd
That the man who was dying beside him
Was God. And blindly he said:

*Remember me when thou comest
Into thy kingdom,* and from the terrible cross
The unimaginable voice
Which one day will judge us all

Promised him Paradise. Nothing more was said
Between them before the end came,
But history will not let the memory
Of their last afternoon die.

O friends, the innocence of this friend
Of Jesus! That simplicity which made him,
From the disgrace of punishment, ask for
And be granted Paradise

Was what drove him time
And again to sin and to bloody crime.

[*Mark Strand*]

ARTE POETICA

Mirar el río hecho de tiempo y agua
Y recordar que el tiempo es otro río,
Saber que nos perdemos como el río
Y que los rostros pasan como el agua.

Sentir que la vigilia es otro sueño
Que sueña no soñar y que la muerte
Que teme nuestra carne es esa muerte
De cada noche, que se llama sueño.

Ver en el día o en el año un símbolo
De los días del hombre y de sus años,
Convertir el ultraje de los años
En una música, un rumor y un símbolo,

Ver en la muerte el sueño, en el ocaso
Un triste oro, tal es la poesía
Que es inmortal y pobre. La poesía
Vuelve como la aurora y el ocaso.

A veces en las tardes una cara
Nos mira desde el fondo de un espejo;
El arte debe ser como ese espejo
Que nos revela nuestra propia cara.

Cuentan que Ulises, harto de prodigios,
Lloró de amor al divisar su Itaca
Verde y humilde. El arte es esa Itaca
De verde eternidad, no de prodigios.

También es como el río interminable
Que pasa y queda y es cristal de un mismo
Heráclito inconstante, que es el mismo
Y es otro, como el río interminable.

ARS POETICA

To look at the river made of time and water
And remember that time is another river,
To know that we are lost like the river
And that faces dissolve like water.

To be aware that waking dreams it is not asleep
While it is another dream, and that the death
That our flesh goes in fear of is that death
Which comes every night and is called sleep.

To see in the day or in the year a symbol
Of the days of man and of his years,
To transmute the outrage of the years
Into a music, a murmur of voices, and a symbol,

To see in death sleep, and in the sunset
A sad gold—such is poetry,
Which is immortal and poor. Poetry
Returns like the dawn and the sunset.

At times in the evenings a face
Looks at us out of the depths of a mirror;
Art should be like that mirror
Which reveals to us our own face.

They say that Ulysses, sated with marvels,
Wept tears of love at the sight of his Ithaca,
Green and humble. Art is that Ithaca
Of green eternity, not of marvels.

It is also like the river with no end
That flows and remains and is the mirror of one same
Inconstant Heraclitus, who is the same
And is another, like the river with no end.

[*W. S. Merwin*]

UNA ROSA Y MILTON

De las generaciones de las rosas
Que en el fondo del tiempo se han perdido
Quiero que una se salve del olvido,
Una sin marca o signo entre las cosas
Que fueron. El destino me depara
Este don de nombrar por vez primera
Esa flor silenciosa, la postrera
Rosa que Milton acercó a su cara,
Sin verla. Oh tú, bermeja o amarilla
O blanca rosa de un jardín borrado,
Deja mágicamente tu pasado
Inmemorial y en este verso brilla,
Oro, sangre o marfil o tenebrosa
Como en sus manos, invisible rosa.

A ROSE AND MILTON

From all the generations of past roses,
Disintegrated in the depths of time,
I want one to be spared oblivion—
One unexceptional rose from all the things
Which once existed. Destiny allows me
The privilege of choosing, this first time,
That silent flower, the very final rose
That Milton held before his face, but could
Not see. O rose, vermilion or yellow
Or white, from some obliterated garden,
Your past existence magically lasts
And glows forever in this poetry,
Gold or blood-colored, ivory or shadowed,
As once in Milton's hands, invisible rose.

[*Alastair Reid*]

A QUIEN YA NO ES JOVEN

Ya puedes ver el trágico escenario
Y cada cosa en el lugar debido;
La espada y la ceniza para Dido
Y la moneda para Belisario.
¿A qué sigues buscando en el brumoso
Bronce de los hexámetros la guerra
Si están aquí los siete pies de tierra,
La brusca sangre y el abierto foso?
Aquí te acecha el insondable espejo
Que soñará y olvidará el reflejo
De tus postrimerías y agonías.
Ya te cerca lo último. Es la casa
Donde tu lenta y breve tarde pasa
Y la calle que ves todos los días.

TO ONE NO LONGER YOUNG

Already you can see the tragic setting
And each thing there in its appointed place;
The broadsword and the ash destined for Dido,
The coin prepared for Belisarius.
Why do you go on searching in the furtive
Bronze of Greek hexameters for war
When these six feet of ground wait for you here,
The sudden rush of blood, the yawning grave?
Here watching you is the inscrutable glass
Which will dream up and then forget the face
Of all your dwindling days, your agony.
The last one now draws in. It is the house
In which your slow, brief evening comes to pass
And the street front that you look at every day.

[*Alastair Reid*]

ODISEA, LIBRO VIGESIMO TERCERO

Ya la espada de hierro ha ejecutado
La debida labor de la venganza;
Ya los ásperos dardos y la lanza
La sangre del perverso han prodigado.
A despecho de un dios y de sus mares
A su reino y su reina ha vuelto Ulises,
A despecho de un dios y de los grises
Vientos y del estrépito de Ares.
Ya en el amor del compartido lecho
Duerme la clara reina sobre el pecho
De su rey pero ¿dónde está aquel hombre
Que en los días y noches del destierro
Erraba por el mundo como un perro
Y decía que Nadie era su nombre?

ODYSSEY, BOOK TWENTY-THREE

Now has the rapier of iron wrought
The work of justice, and revenge is done.
Now spear and arrows, pitiless every one,
Have made the blood of insolence run out.
For all a god and all his seas could do
Ulysses has returned to realm and queen.
For all a god could do, and the grey-green
Gales and Ares' murderous hullabaloo.
Now in the love of their own bridal bed
The shining queen has fallen asleep, her head
Upon her king's breast. Where is that man now
Who in his exile wandered night and day
Over the world like a wild dog, and would say
His name was No One, No One, anyhow?

[*Robert Fitzgerald*]

A UN POETA MENOR DE 1899

Dejar un verso para la hora triste
Que en el confín del día nos acecha,
Ligar tu nombre a su doliente fecha
De oro y de vaga sombra. Eso quisiste.
¡Con qué pasión, al declinar el día,
Trabajarías el extraño verso
Que, hasta la dispersión del universo,
La hora de extraño azul confirmaría!
No sé si lo lograste ni siquiera,
Vago hermano mayor, si has existido,
Pero estoy solo y quiero que el olvido
Restituya a los días tu ligera
Sombra para este ya cansado alarde
De unas palabras en que esté la tarde.

TO A MINOR POET OF 1899

To leave behind a verse for that sad hour
Lying in wait for us at the day's close,
To link your name with its fading gold
And lengthening shadow: that was your desire.
With what passion when the day was through
You labored over that strange line, which would,
Until the dissolution of the world,
Affirm that special hour and its strange blue!
Whether you found it, I don't know, or even,
Vague elder brother, whether you were real,
But I'm alone, I wish oblivion
Would give your weightless ghost back to the days
To aid this weary word-show that designs
To hold the evening fixed within its lines.

[*William Ferguson*]

TEXAS

Aquí también. Aquí, como en el otro
Confín del continente, el infinito
Campo en que muere solitario el grito;
Aquí también el indio, el lazo, el potro.
Aquí también el pájaro secreto
Que sobre los fragores de la historia
Canta para una tarde y su memoria;
Aquí también el místico alfabeto
De los astros, que hoy dictan a mi cálamo
Nombres que el incesante laberinto
De los días no arrastra: San Jacinto
Y esas otras Termópilas, el Alamo.
Aquí también esa desconocida
Y ansiosa y breve cosa que es la vida.

TEXAS

Here too. Here as at the other edge
Of the hemisphere, an endless plain
Where a man's cry dies a lonely death.
Here too the Indian, the lasso, the wild horse.
Here too the bird that never shows itself,
That sings for the memory of one evening
Over the rumblings of history;
Here too the mystic alphabet of stars
Leading my pen over the page to names
Not swept aside in the continual
Labyrinth of days: San Jacinto
And that other Thermopylae, the Alamo.
Here too the never understood,
Anxious, and brief affair that is life.

[*Mark Strand*]

COMPOSICION ESCRITA
EN UN EJEMPLAR DE LA GESTA
DE BEOWULF

A veces me pregunto qué razones
Me mueven a estudiar sin esperanza
De precisión, mientras mi noche avanza,
La lengua de los ásperos sajones.
Gastada por los años la memoria
Deja caer la en vano repetida
Palabra y es así como mi vida
Teje y desteje su cansada historia.
Será (me digo entonces) que de un modo
Secreto y suficiente el alma sabe
Que es inmortal y que su vasto y grave
Círculo abarca todo y puede todo.
Más allá de este afán y de este verso
Me aguarda inagotable el universo.

POEM WRITTEN
IN A COPY
OF BEOWULF

At various times I have asked myself what reasons
Moved me to study while my night came down,
Without particular hope of satisfaction,
The language of the blunt-tongued Anglo-Saxons.
Used up by the years my memory
Loses its grip on words that I have vainly
Repeated and repeated. My life in the same way
Weaves and unweaves its weary history.
Then I tell myself: it must be that the soul
Has some secret sufficient way of knowing
That it is immortal, that its vast encompassing
Circle can take in all, can accomplish all.
Beyond my anxiety and beyond this writing
The universe waits, inexhaustible, inviting.

[*Alastair Reid*]

HENGEST CYNING

EPITAFIO DEL REY

Bajo la piedra yace el cuerpo de Hengist
Que fundó en estas islas el primer reino
De la estirpe de Odín
Y sació el hambre de las águilas.

HABLA EL REY

No sé qué runas habrá marcado el hierro en la
    piedra
Pero mis palabras son éstas:
Bajo los cielos yo fui Hengist el mercenario.
Vendí mi fuerza y mi coraje a los reyes
De las regiones del ocaso que lindan
Con el mar que se llama
El Guerrero Armado de Lanza,
Pero la fuerza y el coraje no sufren
Que las vendan los hombres
Y así, después de haber acuchillado en el Norte
A los enemigos del rey britano,
Le quité la luz y la vida.
Me place el reino que gané con la espada;
Hay ríos para el remo y para la red
Y largos veranos
Y tierra para el arado y para la hacienda
Y britanos para trabajarla
Y ciudades de piedra que entregaremos
A la desolación,
Porque las habitan los muertos.
Yo sé que a mis espaldas
Me tildan de traidor los britanos,
Pero yo he sido fiel a mi valentía
Y no he confiado mi destino a los otros
Y ningún hombre se animó a traicionarme.

HENGEST CYNING

Beneath this stone lies the body of Hengist
Who founded in these islands the first kingdom
Of the royal house of Odin
And glutted the screaming eagle's greed.

THE KING SPEAKS

I know not what runes will be scraped on the stone
But my words are these:
Beneath the heavens I was Hengist the mercenary.
My might and my courage I marketed to kings
Whose lands lay west over the water
Here at the edge of the sea
Called the Spear-Warrior;
But a man's might and his courage can
Not long bear being sold,
And so after cutting down all through the North
The foes of the Briton king,
From him too I took light and life together.
I like this kingdom that I seized with my sword;
It has rivers for the net and the oar
And long seasons of sun
And soil for the plough and for husbandry
And Britons for working the farms
And cities of stone which we shall allow
To crumble to ruin,
Because there dwell the ghosts of the dead.
But behind my back I know
These Britons brand me traitor,
Yet I have been true to my deeds and my daring
And to other men's care never yielded my destiny
And no one dared ever betray me.

[*Norman Thomas di Giovanni*]

FRAGMENTO

Una espada,
Una espada de hierro forjada en el frío del alba,
Una espada con runas
Que nadie podrá desoír ni descifrar del todo,
Una espada del Báltico que será cantada en
    Nortumbria,
Una espada que los poetas
Igualarán al hielo y al fuego,
Una espada que un rey dará a otro rey
Y este rey a un sueño,
Una espada que será leal
Hasta una hora que ya sabe el Destino,
Una espada que iluminará la batalla.

Una espada para la mano
Que regirá la hermosa batalla, el tejido de hombres,
Una espada para la mano
Que enrojecerá los dientes del lobo
Y el despiadado pico del cuervo,
Una espada para la mano
Que prodigará el oro rojo,
Una espada para la mano
Que dará muerte a la serpiente en su lecho de oro,
Una espada para la mano
Que ganará un reino y perderá un reino,
Una espada para la mano
Que derribará la selva de lanzas.
Una espada para la mano de Beowulf.

FRAGMENT

A sword,
An iron sword hammered out in the cold of dawn,
A sword carved with runes
That no one will overlook, that no one will interpret
    in full,
A sword from the Baltic that will be celebrated in
    Northumbria,
A sword that poets
Will equate to ice and fire,
A sword that will be handed from king to king
And from king to dream,
A sword that will be loyal
To an hour known only to Destiny,
A sword that will light up the battle.

A sword to fit the hand
That will guide the beautiful battle, the web of men,
A sword to fit the hand
That will stain with blood the wolf's fangs
And the raven's ruthless beak,
A sword to fit the hand
That will squander red gold,
A sword to fit the hand
That will deal death to the serpent in its golden lair,
A sword to fit the hand
That will gain a kingdom and lose a kingdom,
A sword to fit the hand
That will bring down the forest of spears.
A sword to fit the hand of Beowulf.

[Norman Thomas di Giovanni]

A UN POETA SAJON

Tú cuya carne que hoy es polvo y planeta
Pesó como la nuestra sobre la tierra,
Tú cuyos ojos vieron el sol, esa famosa estrella,
Tú que viviste no en el rígido ayer
Sino en el incesante presente,
En el último punto y ápice vertiginoso del tiempo,
Tú que en tu monasterio fuiste llamado
Por la antigua voz de la épica,
Tú que tejiste las palabras,
Tú que cantaste la victoria de Brunanburh
Y no la atribuiste al Señor
Sino a la espada de tu rey,
Tú que con júbilo feroz cantaste las espadas de hierro,
La vergüenza del viking,
El festín del cuervo y del águila,
Tú que en la oda militar congregaste
Las rituales metáforas de la estirpe,
Tú que en un tiempo sin historia
Viste en el ahora el ayer
Y en el sudor y sangre de Brunanburh
Un cristal de antiguas auroras,
Tú que tanto querías a tu Inglaterra
Y no la nombraste,
Hoy no eres otra cosa que unas palabras
Que los germanistas anotan.
Hoy no eres otra cosa que mi voz
Cuando revive tus palabras de hierro.

Pido a mis dioses o a la suma del tiempo
Que mis días merezcan el olvido,
Que mi nombre sea Nadie como el de Ulises,
Pero que algún verso perdure
En la noche propicia a la memoria
O en las mañanas de los hombres.

TO A SAXON POET

You whose flesh, now dust and planet,
Once weighed like ours on earth,
Whose eyes took in the sun, that famous star,
You who lived not in the rigid past
But in a ceaseless present
At the topmost point and dizzying apex of time,
Who in your monastery heard the call
Of the epic's ancient voice,
Who wove words
And sang the victory at Brunanburh,
Ascribing it not to God
But to your king's sword edge,
You who with fierce joy celebrated swords hammered
    out of iron,
The Norseman's shame,
The banquet of raven and eagle,
Gathering in your military ode
The ritual metaphors of your kin,
You who in an age without history
Saw in the present the past
And in the blood and sweat of Brunanburh
A mirror of ancient sunrises,
You who so much loved your England
And did not name her—
Today you are but a few words
That Germanic scholars annotate;
Today you are my voice
When it calls back to life your iron words.

Of my gods or of the sum of time I ask
That my days attain oblivion,
That like Ulysses I may be called No One,
But that some verse of mine survive
On a night favorable to memory
Or in the mornings of men.

[*Norman Thomas di Giovanni*]

[161]

SNORRI STURLUSON (1179–1241)

Tú, que legaste una mitología
De hielo y fuego a la filial memoria,
Tú, que fijaste la violenta gloria
De tu estirpe germánica y bravía,
Sentiste con asombro en una tarde
De espadas que tu triste carne humana
Temblaba. En esa tarde sin mañana
Te fue dado saber que eras cobarde.
En la noche de Islandia, la salobre
Borrasca mueve el mar. Está cercada
Tu casa. Has bebido hasta las heces
El deshonor inolvidable. Sobre
Tu pálida cabeza cae la espada
Como en tu libro cayó tantas veces.

SNORRI STURLUSON (1179–1241)

You, who bequeathed a mythology
Of ice and fire to filial recall,
Who chronicled the violent glory
Of your defiant Germanic stock,
Discovered in amazement one night
Of swords that your untrustworthy flesh
Trembled. On that night without sequel
You realized you were a coward. . . .
In the darkness of Iceland the salt
Wind moves the mounting sea. Your house is
Surrounded. You have drunk to the dregs
Unforgettable dishonor. On
Your head, your sickly face, falls the sword
As it fell so often in your book.

[*Richard Howard and César Rennert*]

A CARLOS XII

Viking de las estepas, Carlos doce
De Suecia, que cumpliste aquel camino
Del Septentrión al Sur de tu divino
Antecesor Odín, fueron tu goce

Los trabajos que mueven la memoria
De los hombres al canto, la batalla
Mortal, el duro horror de la metralla,
La firme espada y la sangrienta gloria.

Supiste que vencer o ser vencido
Son caras de un Azar indiferente,
Que no hay otra virtud que ser valiente

Y que el mármol, al fin, será el olvido.
Ardes glacial, más solo que el desierto;
Nadie llegó a tu alma y ya estás muerto.

TO CHARLES XII OF SWEDEN

Viking of the steppes, who followed
That road from North to South of your
Divine ancestor Odin, such
Were your delights: the deeds that move

The memory of men to song,
Mortal combat, the hard horror
Of grapeshot, the sudden sword and
Bloody fame. You knew that success

And defeat are faces of Chance,
The Indifferent; that there is no
Virtue but valor: a statue

Is no more than oblivion.
Arctic, ablaze, alone, no one
Reached your soul and now you are dead.

[*Richard Howard and César Rennert*]

EMANUEL SWEDENBORG

Más alto que los otros, caminaba
Aquel hombre lejano entre los hombres;
Apenas si llamaba por sus nombres
Secretos a los ángeles. Miraba
Lo que no ven los ojos terrenales:
La ardiente geometría, el cristalino
Laberinto de Dios y el remolino
Sórdido de los goces infernales.
Sabía que la Gloria y el Averno
En tu alma están y sus mitologías;
Sabía, como el griego, que los días
Del tiempo son espejos del Eterno.
En árido latín fue registrando
Ultimas cosas sin por qué ni cuando.

EMANUEL SWEDENBORG

Taller than the others, this man
Walked, among them, at a distance,
Now and then calling the angels
By their secret names. He would see
That which earthly eyes do not see:
The fierce geometry, the crystal
Labyrinth of God and the sordid
Milling of infernal delights.
He knew that Glory and Hell too
Are in your soul, with all their myths;
He knew, like the Greek, that the days
Of time are Eternity's mirrors.
In dry Latin he went on listing
The unconditional Last Things.

[*Richard Howard and César Rennert*]

JONATHAN EDWARDS (1703–1758)

Lejos de la ciudad, lejos del foro
Clamoroso y del tiempo, que es mudanza,
Edwards, eterno ya, sueña y avanza
A la sombra de árboles de oro.
Hoy es mañana y es ayer. No hay una
Cosa de Dios en el sereno ambiente
Que no lo exalte misteriosamente,
El oro de la tarde o de la luna.
Piensa feliz que el mundo es un eterno
Instrumento de ira y que el ansiado
Cielo para unos pocos fue creado
Y casi para todos el infierno.
En el centro puntual de la maraña
Hay otro prisionero, Dios, la Araña.

JONATHAN EDWARDS (1703–1758)

Far from the Common, far from the loud
City and from time, which is change,
Edwards dreams, eternal now, and comes
Into the shadow of golden trees. Today
Is tomorrow and yesterday. Not one
Thing of God's in the motionless world
Fails to exalt him strangely—the gold
Of the evening, or of the moon.
Content, he knows the world is an eternal
Vessel of wrath and that the coveted
Heaven was created for a few
And Hell for almost all. Exactly
In the center of the web there is
Another prisoner, God, the Spider.

[*Richard Howard and César Rennert*]

EMERSON

Ese alto caballero americano
Cierra el volumen de Montaigne y sale
En busca de otro goce que no vale
Menos, la tarde que ya exalta el llano.
Hacia el hondo poniente y su declive,
Hacia el confín que ese poniente dora,
Camina por los campos como ahora
Por la memoria de quien esto escribe.
Piensa: Leí los libros esenciales
Y otros compuse que el oscuro olvido
No ha de borrar. Un dios me ha concedido
Lo que es dado saber a los mortales.
Por todo el continente anda mi nombre;
No he vivido. Quisiera ser otro hombre.

EMERSON

Closing the heavy volume of Montaigne,
The tall New Englander goes out
Into an evening which exalts the fields.
It is a pleasure worth no less than reading.
He walks toward the final sloping of the sun,
Toward the landscape's gilded edge;
He moves through darkening fields as he moves now
Through the memory of the one who writes this down.
He thinks: I have read the essential books
And written others which oblivion
Will not efface. I have been allowed
That which is given mortal man to know.
The whole continent knows my name.
I have not lived. I want to be someone else.

[*Mark Strand*]

EDGAR ALLAN POE

Pompas del mármol, negra anatomía
Que ultrajan los gusanos sepulcrales,
Del triunfo de la muerte los glaciales
Símbolos congregó. No los temía.
Temía la otra sombra, la amorosa,
Las comunes venturas de la gente;
No lo cegó el metal resplandeciente
Ni el mármol sepulcral sino la rosa.
Como del otro lado del espejo
Se entregó solitario a su complejo
Destino de inventor de pesadillas.
Quizá, del otro lado de la muerte,
Sigue erigiendo solitario y fuerte
Espléndidas y atroces maravillas.

EDGAR ALLAN POE

Marble splendors, black anatomy
Slandered by the worm in the winding sheet—
All the cold symbols he collected
Of death's victory. And feared them not.
What he feared was that other shadow,
Love's, the usual happiness of
Most People; he was not blinded by
Burnished metal or marble, but by the rose.
As if on the wrong side of the mirror,
He yielded, solitary, to his rich
Fate of fabricating nightmares. Perhaps,
On the wrong side of death, solitary
And unyielding, he devises more
Magnificent and atrocious marvels still.

[*Richard Howard and César Rennert*]

CAMDEN, 1892

El olor del café y de los periódicos.
El domingo y su tedio. La mañana
Y en la entrevista página esa vana
Publicación de versos alegóricos
De un colega feliz. El hombre viejo
Está postrado y blanco en su decente
Habitación de pobre. Ociosamente
Mira su cara en el cansado espejo.
Piensa, ya sin asombro, que esa cara
Es él. La distraída mano toca
La turbia barba y la saqueada boca.
No está lejos el fin. Su voz declara:
Casi no soy, pero mis versos ritman
La vida y su esplendor. Yo fui Walt Whitman.

CAMDEN 1892

The fragrance of coffee and newspapers.
Sunday and its tedium. This morning,
On the uninvestigated page, that vain
Column of allegorical verses
By a happy colleague. The old man lies
Prostrate, pale, even white in his decent
Room, the room of a poor man. Needlessly
He glances at his face in the exhausted
Mirror. He thinks, without surprise now,
That face is me. One fumbling hand touches
The tangled beard, the devastated mouth.
The end is not far off. His voice declares:
I am almost gone. But my verses scan
Life and its splendor. I was Walt Whitman.

[*Richard Howard and César Rennert*]

PARIS, 1856

La larga postración lo ha acostumbrado
A anticipar la muerte. Le daría
Miedo salir al clamoroso día
Y andar entre los hombres. Derribado,
Enrique Heine piensa en aquel río,
El tiempo, que lo aleja lentamente
De esa larga penumbra y del doliente
Destino de ser hombre y ser judío.
Piensa en las delicadas melodías
Cuyo instrumento fue, pero bien sabe
Que el trino no es del árbol ni del ave
Sino del tiempo y de sus vagos días.
No han de salvarte, no, tus ruiseñores,
Tus noches de oro y tus cantadas flores.

PARIS 1856

A long prostration has addicted him
To presuming on death: he would not dare
Enter the chattering daylight now
And venture among men. Broken, unhinged,
Heinrich Heine thinks of that slow river
Time, which ferries him across the long
Dimness and which divides him from
The painful fate of being a man,
A Jew. He thinks of the fragile songs
Whose instrument he was, although he knows
The tune is not the tree's, and not the bird's—
The tune is time's and comes from his pale days.
    They cannot save you, your larks, your doves,
    Nor all your golden nights and famous flowers.

[Richard Howard and César Rennert]

RAFAEL CANSINOS-ASSENS

La imagen de aquel pueblo lapidado
Y execrado, inmortal en su agonía,
En las negras vigilias lo atraía
Con una suerte de terror sagrado.
Bebió como quien bebe un hondo vino
Los Salmos y el Cantar de la Escritura
Y sintió que era suya esa dulzura
Y sintió que era suyo aquel destino.
Lo llamaba Israel. Intimamente
La oyó Cansinos como oyó el profeta
En la secreta cumbre la secreta
Voz del Señor desde la zarza ardiente.
Acompáñeme siempre su memoria;
Las otras cosas las dirá la gloria.

RAFAEL CANSINOS-ASSENS

The image of such a people, detested
And stoned, and in their suffering eternal,
In all the blackness of their fearful vigil
Drew him on with a kind of holy dread.
As with deep drinks of vintage, so did he
Drink the Psalms and the Song of Solomon;
He felt that such a sweetness was his own,
He felt that all this was his destiny.
Israel called him. And Cansinos heard
Her intimately, as Moses the prophet
Heard at the secret summit the secret word
Of the Lord talking from the burning thicket.
Then let his memory walk with me forever;
And all the rest of it glory will tell of.

[*John Hollander*]

LOS ENIGMAS

Yo que soy el que ahora está cantando
Seré mañana el misterioso, el muerto,
El morador de un mágico y desierto
Orbe sin antes ni después ni cuando.
Así afirma la mística. Me creo
Indigno del Infierno o de la Gloria,
Pero nada predigo. Nuestra historia
Cambia como las formas de Proteo.
¿Qué errante laberinto, qué blancura
Ciega de resplandor será mi suerte,
Cuando me entregue el fin de esta aventura
La curiosa experiencia de la muerte?
Quiero beber su cristalino Olvido,
Ser para siempre; pero no haber sido.

THE ENIGMAS

I who am singing these lines today
Will be tomorrow the enigmatic corpse
Who dwells in a realm, magical and barren,
Without a before or an after or a when.
So say the mystics. I say I believe
Myself undeserving of Heaven or of Hell,
But make no predictions. Each man's tale
Shifts like the watery forms of Proteus.
What errant labyrinth, what blinding flash
Of splendor and glory shall become my fate
When the end of this adventure presents me with
The curious experience of death?
I want to drink its crystal-pure oblivion,
To be forever; but never to have been.

[*John Updike*]

A QUIEN ESTA LEYENDOME

Eres invulnerable. ¿No te han dado
Los númenes que rigen tu destino
Certidumbre de polvo? ¿No es acaso
Tu irreversible tiempo el de aquel río
En cuyo espejo Heráclito vio el símbolo
De su fugacidad? Te espera el mármol
Que no leerás. En él ya están escritos
La fecha, la ciudad y el epitafio.
Sueños del tiempo son también los otros,
No firme bronce ni acendrado oro;
El universo es, como tú, Proteo.
Sombra, irás a la sombra que te aguarda
Fatal en el confín de tu jornada;
Piensa que de algún modo ya estás muerto.

TO MY READER

You are invulnerable. Have they not shown you,
The powers that preordain your destiny,
The certainty of dust? Is not your time
As irreversible as that same river
Where Heraclitus, mirrored, saw the symbol
Of fleeting life? A marble slab awaits you
Which you will not read—on it, already written,
The date, the city, and the epitaph.
Other men too are only dreams of time,
Not everlasting bronze nor shining gold;
The universe is, like you, a Proteus.
Dark, you will enter the darkness that expects you,
Doomed to the limits of your traveled time.
Know that in some sense you by now are dead.

[*Alastair Reid*]

ALGUIEN

Un hombre trabajado por el tiempo,
un hombre que ni siquiera espera la muerte
(las pruebas de la muerte son estadísticas
y nadie hay que no corra el albur
de ser el primer inmortal),
un hombre que ha aprendido a agradecer
las modestas limosnas de los días:
el sueño, la rutina, el sabor del agua,
una no sospechada etimología,
un verso latino o sajón,
la memoria de una mujer que lo ha abandonado
hace ya tantos años
que hoy puede recordarla sin amargura,
un hombre que no ignora que el presente
ya es el porvenir y el olvido,
un hombre que ha sido desleal
y con el que fueron desleales,
puede sentir de pronto, al cruzar la calle,
una misteriosa felicidad
que no viene del lado de la esperanza
sino de una antigua inocencia,
de su propia raíz o de un dios disperso.

Sabe que no debe mirarla de cerca,
porque hay razones más terribles que tigres
que le demostrarán su obligación
de ser un desdichado,
pero humildemente recibe
esa felicidad, esa ráfaga.

Quizá en la muerte para siempre seremos,
cuando el polvo sea polvo,
esa indescifrable raíz,
de la cual para siempre crecerá,
ecuánime o atroz,
nuestro solitario cielo o infierno.

SOMEONE

A man worn down by time,
a man who does not even expect death
(the proofs of death are statistics
and everyone runs the risk
of being the first immortal),
a man who has learned to express thanks
for the days' modest alms:
sleep, routine, the taste of water,
an unsuspected etymology,
a Latin or Saxon verse,
the memory of a woman who left him
thirty years ago now
whom he can call to mind without bitterness,
a man who is aware that the present
is both future and oblivion,
a man who has betrayed
and has been betrayed,
may feel suddenly, when crossing the street,
a mysterious happiness
not coming from the side of hope
but from an ancient innocence,
from his own root or from some diffused god.

He knows better than to look at it closely,
for there are reasons more terrible than tigers
which will prove to him
that wretchedness is his duty,
but he accepts humbly
this felicity, this glimmer.

Perhaps in death when the dust
is dust, we will be forever
this undecipherable root,
from which will grow forever,
serene or horrible,
our solitary heaven or hell.

[*W. S. Merwin*]

EVERNESS

Sólo una cosa no hay. Es el olvido.
Dios, que salva el metal, salva la escoria
Y cifra en Su profética memoria
Las lunas que serán y las que han sido.
Ya todo está. Los miles de reflejos
Que entre los dos crepúsculos del día
Tu rostro fue dejando en los espejos
Y los que irá dejando todavía.
Y todo es una parte del diverso
Cristal de esa memoria, el universo;
No tienen fin sus arduos corredores
Y las puertas se cierran a tu paso;
Sólo del otro lado del ocaso
Verás los Arquetipos y Esplendores.

EVERNESS

One thing does not exist: Oblivion.
God saves the metal and he saves the dross,
And his prophetic memory guards from loss
The moons to come, and those of evenings gone.
Everything *is*: the shadows in the glass
Which, in between the day's two twilights, you
Have scattered by the thousands, or shall strew
Henceforward in the mirrors that you pass.
And everything is part of that diverse
Crystalline memory, the universe;
Whoever through its endless mazes wanders
Hears door on door click shut behind his stride,
And only from the sunset's farther side
Shall view at last the Archetypes and the Splendors.

[*Richard Wilbur*]

EWIGKEIT

Torne en mi boca el verso castellano
A decir lo que siempre está diciendo
Desde el latín de Séneca: el horrendo
Dictamen de que todo es del gusano.
Torne a cantar la pálida ceniza,
Los fastos de la muerte y la victoria
De esa reina retórica que pisa
Los estandartes de la vanagloria.
No así. Lo que mi barro ha bendecido
No lo voy a negar como un cobarde.
Sé que una cosa no hay. Es el olvido;
Sé que en la eternidad perdura y arde
Lo mucho y lo precioso que he perdido:
Esa fragua, esa luna y esa tarde.

EWIGKEIT

Turn on my tongue, O Spanish verse; confirm
Once more what Spanish verse has always said
Since Seneca's black Latin; speak your dread
Sentence that all is fodder for the worm.
Come, celebrate once more pale ash, pale dust,
The pomps of death and the triumphant crown
Of that bombastic queen who tramples down
The petty banners of our pride and lust.
Enough of that. What things have blessed my clay
Let me not cravenly deny. The one
Word of no meaning is Oblivion,
And havened in eternity, I know,
My many precious losses burn and stay:
That forge, that night, that risen moon aglow.

[*Richard Wilbur*]

EDIPO Y EL ENIGMA

Cuadrúpedo en la aurora, alto en el día
Y con tres pies errando por el vano
Ambito de la tarde, así veía
La eterna esfinge a su inconstante hermano,
El hombre, y con la tarde un hombre vino
Qué descifró aterrado en el espejo
De la monstruosa imagen, el reflejo
De su declinación y su destino.
Somos Edipo y de un eterno modo
La larga y triple bestia somos, todo
Lo que seremos y lo que hemos sido.
Nos aniquilaría ver la ingente
Forma de nuestro ser; piadosamente
Dios nos depara sucesión y olvido.

OEDIPUS AND THE RIDDLE

At dawn four-footed, at midday erect,
And wandering on three legs in the deserted
Spaces of afternoon, thus the eternal
Sphinx had envisioned her changing brother
Man, and with afternoon there came a person
Deciphering, appalled at the monstrous other
Presence in the mirror, the reflection
Of his decay and of his destiny.
We are Oedipus; in some eternal way
We are the long and threefold beast as well—
All that we will be, all that we have been.
It would annihilate us all to see
The huge shape of our being; mercifully
God offers us issue and oblivion.

[*John Hollander*]

SPINOZA

Las traslúcidas manos del judío
Labran en la penumbra los cristales
Y la tarde que muere es miedo y frío.
(Las tardes a las tardes son iguales.)
Las manos y el espacio de jacinto
Que palidece en el confín del Ghetto
Casi no existen para el hombre quieto
Que está soñando un claro laberinto.
No lo turba la fama, ese reflejo
De sueños en el sueño de otro espejo,
Ni el temeroso amor de las doncellas.
Libre de la metáfora y del mito
Labra un arduo cristal: el infinito
Mapa de Aquél que es todas Sus estrellas.

SPINOZA

The Jew's hands, translucent in the dusk,
Polish the lenses time and again.
The dying afternoon is fear, is
Cold, and all afternoons are the same.
The hands and the hyacinth-blue air
That whitens at the Ghetto edges
Do not quite exist for this silent
Man who conjures up a clear labyrinth—
Undisturbed by fame, that reflection
Of dreams in the dream of another
Mirror, nor by maidens' timid love.
Free of metaphor and myth, he grinds
A stubborn crystal: the infinite
Map of the One who is all His stars.

[*Richard Howard and César Rennert*]

ADAM CAST FORTH

¿Hubo un Jardín o fue el Jardín un sueño?
Lento en la vaga luz, me he preguntado,
Casi como un consuelo, si el pasado
De que este Adán, hoy mísero, era dueño,
No fue sino una mágica impostura
De aquel Dios que soñé. Ya es impreciso
En la memoria el claro Paraíso,
Pero yo sé que existe y que perdura,
Aunque no para mí. La terca tierra
Es mi castigo y la incestuosa guerra
De Caínes y Abeles y su cría.
Y, sin embargo, es mucho haber amado,
Haber sido feliz, haber tocado
El viviente Jardín, siquiera un día.

ADAM CAST FORTH

The Garden—was it real or was it dream?
Slow in the hazy light, I have been asking,
Almost as a comfort, if the past
Belonging to this now unhappy Adam
Was nothing but a magic fantasy
Of that God I dreamed. Now it is imprecise
In memory, that lucid paradise,
But I know it exists and will persist
Though not for me. The unforgiving earth
Is my affliction, and the incestuous wars
Of Cains and Abels and their progeny.
Nevertheless, it means much to have loved,
To have been happy, to have touched upon
The living Garden, even for one day.

[*Alastair Reid*]

A UNA MONEDA

Fría y tormentosa la noche que zarpé de
  Montevideo.
Al doblar el Cerro,
tiré desde la cubierta más alta
una moneda que brilló y se anegó en las aguas
  barrosas,
una cosa de luz que arrebataron el tiempo y la
  tiniebla.
Tuve la sensación de haber cometido un acto
  irrevocable,
de agregar a la historia del planeta
dos series incesantes, paralelas, quizá infinitas:
mi destino, hecho de zozobra, de amor y de vanas
  vicisitudes,
y el de aquel disco de metal
que las aguas darían al blando abismo
o a los remotos mares que aun roen
despojos del sajón y del viking.
A cada instante de mi sueño o de mi vigilia
corresponde otro de la ciega moneda.
A veces he sentido remordimiento
y otras, envidia,
de ti que estás, como nosotros, en el tiempo y su
  laberinto
y que no lo sabes.

TO A COIN

Cold and storm-threatening the night I sailed from
  Montevideo.
Coming round the Cerro,
I flung a coin from the upper deck
and watched it flash, then sink into the murk below—
a thing of light swallowed up by time and darkness.
And through me went a sensation of having committed
  an irrevocable act,
of adding to the history of the planet
two incessant, parallel, and perhaps infinite series:
my own destiny, compounded of anxieties and love and
  pointless struggles,
and the destiny of that metal disk
which would be borne by tides into the soft chasm
or out to remote seas still silently gnawing
at Saxon or Viking spoils.
Each moment of my sleep or my waking
is matched by another of the blind coin's.
At times I have felt remorse,
at times, envy,
of you, like us, walled in by time and its labyrinth
without knowing it.

[*Norman Thomas di Giovanni*]

OTRO POEMA DE LOS DONES

Gracias quiero dar al divino
Laberinto de los efectos y de las causas
Por la diversidad de las criaturas
Que forman este singular universo,
Por la razón, que no cesará de soñar
Con un plano del laberinto,
Por el rostro de Elena y la perseverancia de Ulises,
Por el amor, que nos deja ver a los otros
Como los ve la divinidad,
Por el firme diamante y el agua suelta,
Por el álgebra, palacio de precisos cristales,
Por las místicas monedas de Angel Silesio,
Por Schopenhauer,
Que acaso descifró el universo,
Por el fulgor del fuego
Que ningún ser humano puede mirar sin un
    asombro antiguo,
Por la caoba, el cedro y el sándalo,
Por el pan y la sal,
Por el misterio de la rosa
Que prodiga color y que no lo ve,
Por ciertas vísperas y días de 1955,
Por los duros troperos que en la llanura
Arrean los animales y el alba,
Por la mañana en Montevideo,
Por el arte de la amistad,
Por el último día de Sócrates,
Por las palabras que en un crepúsculo se dijeron
De una cruz a otra cruz,
Por aquel sueño del Islam que abarcó
Mil noches y una noche,
Por aquel otro sueño del infierno,
De la torre del fuego que purifica
Y de las esferas gloriosas,
Por Swedenborg,

ANOTHER POEM OF GIFTS

I want to give thanks to the divine
Labyrinth of causes and effects
For the diversity of beings
That form this singular universe,
For Reason, that will never give up its dream
Of a map of the labyrinth,
For Helen's face and the perseverance of Ulysses,
For love, which lets us see others
As God sees them,
For the solid diamond and the flowing water,
For Algebra, a palace of exact crystals,
For the mystic coins of Angelus Silesius,
For Schopenhauer,
Who perhaps deciphered the universe,
For the blazing of fire,
That no man can look at without an ancient wonder,
For mahogany, cedar, and sandalwood,
For bread and salt,
For the mystery of the rose
That spends all its color and can not see it,
For certain eves and days of 1955,
For the hard riders who, on the plains,
Drive on the cattle and the dawn,
For mornings in Montevideo,
For the art of friendship,
For Socrates' last day,
For the words spoken one twilight
From one cross to another,
For that dream of Islam that embraced
A thousand nights and a night,
For that other dream of Hell,
Of the tower of cleansing fire
And of the celestial spheres,
For Swedenborg,

Que conversaba con los ángeles en las calles de
    Londres,
Por los ríos secretos e inmemoriales
Que convergen en mí,
Por el idioma que, hace siglos, hablé en Nortumbria,
Por la espada y el arpa de los sajones,
Por el mar, que es un desierto resplandeciente
Y una cifra de cosas que no sabemos
Y un epitafio de los vikings,
Por la música verbal de Inglaterra,
Por la música verbal de Alemania,
Por el oro, que relumbra en los versos,
Por el épico invierno,
Por el nombre de un libro que no he leído:
    Gesta Dei per Francos,
Por Verlaine, inocente como los pájaros,
Por el prisma de cristal y la pesa de bronce,
Por las rayas del tigre,
Por las altas torres de San Francisco y de la isla
    de Manhattan,
Por la mañana en Texas,
Por aquel sevillano que redactó la Epístola Moral
Y cuyo nombre, como él hubiera preferido,
    ignoramos,
Por Séneca y Lucano, de Córdoba,
Que antes del español escribieron
Toda la literatura española,
Por el geométrico y bizarro ajedrez,
Por la tortuga de Zenón y el mapa de Royce,
Por el olor medicinal de los eucaliptos,
Por el lenguaje, que puede simular la sabiduría,
Por el olvido, que anula o modifica el pasado,
Por la costumbre,
Que nos repite y nos confirma como un espejo,
Por la mañana, que nos depara la ilusión de un
    principio,
Por la noche, su tiniebla y su astronomía,

Who talked with the angels in London streets,
For the secret and immemorial rivers
That converge in me,
For the language that, centuries ago, I spoke in
    Northumberland,
For the sword and harp of the Saxons,
For the sea, which is a shining desert
And a secret code for things we do not know
And an epitaph for the Norsemen,
For the word music of England,
For the word music of Germany,
For gold, that shines in verses,
For epic winter,
For the title of a book I have not read: *Gesta Dei
    per Francos*,
For Verlaine, innocent as the birds,
For crystal prisms and bronze weights,
For the tiger's stripes,
For the high towers of San Francisco and Manhattan
    Island,
For mornings in Texas,
For that Sevillian who composed the Moral Epistle
And whose name, as he would have wished, we do not
    know,
For Seneca and Lucan, both of Cordova,
Who, before there was Spanish, had written
All Spanish literature,
For gallant, noble, geometric chess,
For Zeno's tortoise and Royce's map,
For the medicinal smell of eucalyptus trees,
For speech, which can be taken for wisdom,
For forgetfulness, which annuls or modifies the past,
For habits,
Which repeat us and confirm us in our image like a
    mirror,
For morning, that gives us the illusion of a new
    beginning,
For night, its darkness and its astronomy,

Por el valor y la felicidad de los otros,
Por la patria, sentida en los jazmines
O en una vieja espada,
Por Whitman y Francisco de Asís, que ya
   escribieron el poema,
Por el hecho de que el poema es inagotable
Y se confunde con la suma de las criaturas
Y no llegará jamás al último verso
Y varía según los hombres,
Por Frances Haslam, que pidió perdón a sus hijos
Por morir tan despacio,
Por los minutos que preceden al sueño,
Por el sueño y la muerte,
Esos dos tesoros ocultos,
Por los íntimos dones que no enumero,
Por la música, misteriosa forma del tiempo.

For the bravery and happiness of others,
For my country, sensed in jasmine flowers
Or in an old sword,
For Whitman and Francis of Assisi, who already wrote
  this poem,
For the fact that the poem is inexhaustible
And becomes one with the sum of all created things
And will never reach its last verse
And varies according to its writers,
For Frances Haslam, who begged her children's pardon
For dying so slowly,
For the minutes that precede sleep,
For sleep and death,
Those two hidden treasures,
For the intimate gifts I do not mention,
For music, that mysterious form of time.

[*Alan Dugan*]

ODA ESCRITA EN 1966

Nadie es la patria. Ni siquiera el jinete
Que, alto en el alba de una plaza desierta,
Rige un corcel de bronce por el tiempo,
Ni los otros que miran desde el mármol,
Ni los que prodigaron su bélica ceniza
Por los campos de América
O dejaron un verso o una hazaña
O la memoria de una vida cabal
En el justo ejercicio de los días.
Nadie es la patria. Ni siquiera los símbolos.

Nadie es la patria. Ni siquiera el tiempo
Cargado de batallas, de espadas y de éxodos
Y de la lenta población de regiones
Que lindan con la aurora y el ocaso,
Y de rostros que van envejeciendo
En los espejos que se empañan
Y de sufridas agonías anónimas
Que duran hasta el alba
Y de la telaraña de la lluvia
Sobre negros jardines.

La patria, amigos, es un acto perpetuo
Como el perpetuo mundo. (Si el Eterno
Espectador dejara de soñarnos
Un solo instante, nos fulminaría,
Blanco y brusco relámpago, Su olvido.)
Nadie es la patria, pero todos debemos
Ser dignos del antiguo juramento
Que prestaron aquellos caballeros
De ser lo que ignoraban, argentinos,
De ser lo que serían por el hecho
De haber jurado en esa vieja casa.
Somos el porvenir de esos varones,
La justificación de aquellos muertos;

ODE WRITTEN IN 1966

No one is the homeland. Not even the rider
High in the dawn in the empty square,
Who guides a bronze steed through time,
Nor those others who look out from marble,
Nor those who squandered their martial ash
Over the plains of America
Or left a verse or an exploit
Or the memory of a life fulfilled
In the careful exercise of their duties.
No one is the homeland. Nor are the symbols.

No one is the homeland. Not even time
Laden with battles, swords, exile after exile,
And with the slow peopling of regions
Stretching into the dawn and the sunset,
And with faces growing older
In the darkening mirrors,
And with anonymous agonies endured
All night until daybreak,
And with the cobweb of rain
Over black gardens.

The homeland, friends, is a continuous act
As the world is continuous. (If the Eternal
Spectator were to cease for one instant
To dream us, the white sudden lightning
Of his oblivion would burn us up.)
No one is the homeland, but we should all
Be worthy of that ancient oath
Which those gentlemen swore—
To be something they didn't know, to be Argentines;
To be what they would be by virtue
Of the oath taken in that old house.
We are the future of those men,
The justification of those dead.

Nuestro deber es la gloriosa carga
Que a nuestra sombra legan esas sombras
Que debemos salvar.

Nadie es la patria, pero todos los somos.
Arda en mi pecho y en el vuestro, incesante,
Ese límpido fuego misterioso.

Our duty is the glorious burden
Bequeathed to our shadow by those shadows;
It is ours to save.

No one is the homeland—it is all of us.
May that clear, mysterious fire burn
Without ceasing, in my breast and yours.

[*W. S. Merwin*]

LINEAS QUE PUDE HABER ESCRITO
Y PERDIDO HACIA 1922

A Odile Barón Supervielle

Silenciosas batallas del ocaso
en arrabales últimos,
siempre antiguas derrotas de una guerra en el cielo,
albas ruinosas que nos llegan
desde el fondo desierto del espacio
como desde el fondo del tiempo,
negros jardines de la lluvia, una esfinge en un libro
que yo tenía miedo de abrir
y cuya imagen vuelve en los sueños,
la corrupción y el eco que seremos,
la luna sobre el mármol,
árboles que se elevan y perduran
como divinidades tranquilas,
la mutua noche y la esperada tarde,
Walt Whitman, cuyo nombre es el universo,
la espada valerosa de un rey
en el silencioso lecho de un río,
los sajones, los árabes y los godos
que, sin saberlo, me engendraron,
¿soy yo esas cosas y las otras
o son llaves secretas y arduas álgebras
de lo que no sabremos nunca?

LINES I MIGHT HAVE WRITTEN
AND LOST AROUND 1922

To Odile Barón Supervielle

Soundless battles of sunset
beyond the ragged edges of the city,
the ancient recurring defeats of a war in heaven,
ruinous white dawns that come for us
out of the empty ends of space
as from the ends of time,
black gardens of rain, a sphinx in a book
I was always afraid to reopen
and whose image comes back in dreams,
the corrupted matter, the echo we shall be,
the moon on marble,
trees that grow up durable
like untroubled gods,
the night shared, the evening awaited,
Walt Whitman, whose name is the universe,
a king's sword useful in battle
lying at the soundless bed of a river,
the Saxons, the Moors, the Goths
who brought me forth unknowing—
am I these things, and others,
or are they secret keys, impossible algebras
of what we shall never know?

[*William Ferguson*]

JUNIN

Soy, pero soy también el otro, el muerto,
El otro de mi sangre y de mi nombre;
Soy un vago señor y soy el hombre
Que detuvo las lanzas del desierto.
Vuelvo a Junín, donde no estuve nunca,
A tu Junín, abuelo Borges. ¿Me oyes,
Sombra o ceniza última, o desoyes
En tu sueño de bronce esta voz trunca?
Acaso buscas por mis vanos ojos
El épico Junín de tus soldados,
El árbol que plantaste, los cercados
Y en el confín la tribu y los despojos.
Te imagino severo, un poco triste.
Quién me dirá cómo eras y quién fuiste.

Junín, 1966

JUNIN

I am myself and I am him today,
The man who died, the man whose blood and name
Are mine: a stranger here, yet with the fame
He won keeping Indian spears at bay.
I come back to this Junín I've never seen,
To your Junín, grandfather Borges. Shadow
Or final ash, do you hear me now or do
You ignore this voice in your bronze sleep?
Perhaps through these useless eyes you seek in me
That epic Junín of old—the cattle raids
On the horizon's edge, the rows of palisades,
Your mounted troops, the place you set a tree.
I picture you as sad and somewhat stern,
But who and what you were I'll never learn.

[*Norman Thomas di Giovanni*]

UN SOLDADO DE LEE (1862)

Lo ha alcanzado una bala en la ribera
De una clara corriente cuyo nombre
Ignora. Cae de boca. (Es verdadera
La historia y más de un hombre fue aquel hombre.)
El aire de oro mueve las ociosas
Hojas de los pinares. La paciente
Hormiga escala el rostro indiferente.
Sube el sol. Ya han cambiado muchas cosas
Y cambiarán sin término hasta cierto
Día del porvenir en que te canto
A ti que, sin la dádiva del llanto,
Caíste como cae un hombre muerto.
No hay un mármol que guarde tu memoria;
Seis pies de tierra son tu oscura gloria.

A SOLDIER UNDER LEE (1862)

A bullet has caught this soldier by the bank
Of some bright-running creek whose name he does
Not know. He drops among the trees face down.
(This story is true: the man was many men.)
The golden air displays the drooping needles
Of the ranks of forest pine. A patient ant
Clumsily climbs the man's unheeding face.
The sun gets high. Already many things
Have changed and more will change, without an end,
Until a certain day when I will write
Of you who died unceremoniously,
Falling in war the way a dead man falls.
No marble marks the place or tells your name;
Six feet of ground are now your shred of fame.

[*Norman Thomas di Giovanni*]

EL MAR

Antes que el sueño (o el terror) tejiera
Mitologías y cosmogonías,
Antes que el tiempo se acuñara en días,
El mar, el siempre mar, ya estaba y era.
¿Quién es el mar? ¿Quién es aquel violento
Y antiguo ser que roe los pilares
De la tierra y es uno y muchos mares
Y abismo y resplandor y azar y viento?
Quien lo mira lo ve por vez primera,
Siempre. Con el asombro que las cosas
Elementales dejan, las hermosas
Tardes, la luna, el fuego de una hoguera.
¿Quién es el mar, quién soy? Lo sabré el día
Ulterior que sucede a la agonía.

THE SEA

Before our human dream (or terror) wove
Mythologies, cosmogonies, and love,
Before time coined its substance into days,
The sea, the always sea, existed: was.
Who is the sea? Who is that violent being,
Violent and ancient, who gnaws the foundations
Of earth? He is both one and many oceans;
He is abyss and splendor, chance and wind.
Who looks on the sea, sees it the first time,
Every time, with the wonder distilled
From elementary things—from beautiful
Evenings, the moon, the leap of a bonfire.
Who is the sea, and who am I? The day
That follows my last agony shall say.

[*John Updike*]

UNA MAÑANA DE 1649

Carlos avanza entre su pueblo. Mira
A izquierda y a derecha. Ha rechazado
Los brazos de la escolta. Liberado
De la necesidad de la mentira,
Sabe que hoy va a la muerte, no al olvido,
Y que es un rey. La ejecución lo espera;
La mañana es atroz y verdadera.
No hay temor en su carne. Siempre ha sido,
A fuer de buen tahur, indiferente.
Ha apurado la vida hasta las heces;
Ahora está solo entre la armada gente.
No lo infama el patíbulo. Los jueces
No son el Juez. Saluda levemente
Y sonríe. Lo ha hecho tantas veces.

A MORNING OF 1649

Charles comes out among his people, looks
Both left and right. Already he has waived
The attendance of an escort. Liberated
From need of lies, he knows this very day
He goes to death, but not to oblivion—
That he is a king. The execution waits;
The morning is both terrible and true.
There is no shiver in his body. He,
Like a good gambler, has always been
Aloof. And he has drunk life to the lees.
Now he moves singly in an armed mob.
The block does not dishonor him. The judges
Are not the Judge. Lightly he nods his head
And smiles. He has done it now so many times.

[*Alastair Reid*]

A UN POETA SAJON

La nieve de Nortumbria ha conocido
Y ha olvidado la huella de tus pasos
Y son innumerables los ocasos
Que entre nosotros, gris hermano, han sido.
Lento en la lenta sombra labrarías
Metáforas de espadas en los mares
Y del horror que mora en los pinares
Y de la soledad que traen los días.
¿Dónde buscar tus rasgos y tu nombre?
Esas son cosas que el antiguo olvido
Guarda. Nunca sabré cómo habrá sido
Cuando sobre la tierra fuiste un hombre.
Seguiste los caminos del destierro;
Ahora sólo eres tu cantar de hierro.

TO A SAXON POET

The snowfalls of Northumbria have known
And have forgotten the imprint of your feet,
And numberless are the suns that now have set
Between your time and mine, my ghostly kinsman.
Slow in the growing shadows you would fashion
Metaphors of swords on the great seas
And of the horror lurking in the pine trees
And of the loneliness the days brought in.
Where can your features and your name be found?
These are things buried in oblivion.
Now I shall never know how it must have been
For you as a living man who walked his ground.
Exiled, you wandered through your lonely ways.
Now you live only in your iron lays.

[*Alastair Reid*]

EL LABERINTO

Zeus no podría desatar las redes
De piedra que me cercan. He olvidado
Los hombres que antes fui; sigo el odiado
Camino de monótonas paredes
Que es mi destino. Rectas galerías
Que se curvan en círculos secretos
Al cabo de los años. Parapetos
Que ha agrietado la usura de los días.
En el pálido polvo he descifrado
Rastros que temo. El aire me ha traído
En las cóncavas tardes un bramido
O el eco de un bramido desolado.
Sé que en la sombra hay Otro, cuya suerte
Es fatigar las largas soledades
Que tejen y destejen este Hades
Y ansiar mi sangre y devorar mi muerte.
Nos buscamos los dos. Ojalá fuera
Este el último día de la espera.

THE LABYRINTH

Zeus, Zeus himself could not undo these nets
Of stone encircling me. My mind forgets
The persons I have been along the way,
The hated way of monotonous walls,
Which is my fate. The galleries seem straight
But curve furtively, forming secret circles
At the terminus of years; and the parapets
Have been worn smooth by the passage of days.
Here, in the tepid alabaster dust,
Are tracks that frighten me. The hollow air
Of evening sometimes brings a bellowing,
Or the echo, desolate, of bellowing.
I know that hidden in the shadows there
Lurks another, whose task is to exhaust
The loneliness that braids and weaves this hell,
To crave my blood, and to fatten on my death.
We seek each other. Oh, if only this
Were the last day of our antithesis!

[*John Updike*]

FOR THE GUITAR

[PARA LAS SEIS CUERDAS]

MILONGA DE
DOS HERMANOS

Traiga cuentos la guitarra
De cuando el fierro brillaba,
Cuentos de truco y de taba,
De cuadreras y de copas,
Cuentos de la Costa Brava
Y el Camino de las Tropas.

Venga una historia de ayer
Que apreciarán los más lerdos;
El destino no hace acuerdos
Y nadie se lo reproche—
Ya estoy viendo que esta noche
Vienen del Sur los recuerdos.

Velay, señores, la historia
De los hermanos Iberra,
Hombres de amor y de guerra
Y en el peligro primeros,
La flor de los cuchilleros
Y ahora los tapa la tierra.

Suelen al hombre perder
La soberbia o la codicia;
También el coraje envicia
A quien le da noche y día—
El que era menor debía
Más muertes a la justicia.

Cuando Juan Iberra vio
Que el menor lo aventajaba,
La paciencia se le acaba
Y le fue tendiendo un lazo.
Le dio muerte de un balazo,
Allá por la Costa Brava.

MILONGA OF
THE TWO BROTHERS

Let the guitar bring us tales
Of when the knives used to flash,
Tales of gambling and of dice,
Horse races and hard drinking,
Tales of the Costa Brava
And of the old Drovers' Trail.

A story of yesterday
Of appeal to all comers;
No deals can be made with fate,
So no one should reproach it—
I'm aware now that tonight
Memories come from the South.

Gentlemen, here's the story
Of the Iberra brothers—
Men of loving and fighting,
The first to rush to danger,
Flower of all knife fighters,
And now they're six feet under.

Things like pride and avarice
Always lead a man astray;
Courage will also corrupt
If pursued both night and day.
The younger of the two had
More killings to his credit.

When Juan Iberra noticed
The younger was way ahead,
His patience reached its limit
And he set a trap for him.
Laid him dead with a bullet
There on the Costa Brava.

Así de manera fiel
Conté la historia hasta el fin;
Es la historia de Caín
Que sigue matando a Abel.

So in a truthful manner
I've told the tale to its end;
It is the story of Cain
Who goes on killing Abel.

[*Norman Thomas di Giovanni*]

MILONGA DE ALBORNOZ

Alguien ya contó los días,
Alguien ya sabe la hora,
Alguien para Quien no hay
Ni premuras ni demora.

Albornoz pasa silbando
Una milonga entrerriana;
Bajo el ala del chambergo
Sus ojos ven la mañana,

La mañana de este día
Del ochocientos noventa;
En el bajo del Retiro
Ya le han perdido la cuenta

De amores y de trucadas
Hasta el alba y de entreveros
A fierro con los sargentos,
Con propios y forasteros.

Se la tienen bien jurada
Más de un taura y más de un pillo;
En una esquina del Sur
Lo está esperando un cuchillo.

No un cuchillo sino tres,
Antes de clarear el día,
Se le vinieron encima
Y el hombre se defendía.

Un acero entró en el pecho,
Ni se le movió la cara;
Alejo Albornoz murió
Como si no le importara.

MILONGA OF ALBORNOZ

Someone had measured out his time,
Someone marked his day,
Someone to Whom no heed is paid
Either hurry or delay.

Albornoz strolls lightly whistling
An Entre Ríos milonga;
Under the brim of his cocky hat
His eyes take in the morning—

The morning of this day far back
In eighteen ninety-one.
Along the northern waterfront
By now they've lost the sum

Of the loves he had, and cardgames played
Around the clock, or frays
With knives, battling neighbors or cops
Or men he didn't know.

More than one tough, more than one crook
Have had an eye on him;
Somewhere on a Southside street
A knife awaits the man.

Not just a single knife but three,
Before the day grows light;
They came at him behind his back
And he stood firm to fight.

A blade sank deep into his chest—
On his face no pain or dread.
As if it could not matter to him
Alejo Albornoz fell dead.

Pienso que le gustaría
Saber que hoy anda su historia
En una milonga. El tiempo
Es olvido y es memoria.

I think he might have been pleased to know
His tale is told today
In a milonga's lines. Time is
Oblivion and memory.

[*Norman Thomas di Giovanni*]

MUSEUM

[MUSEO]

CUARTETA

Murieron otros, pero ello aconteció en el pasado,
Que es la estación (nadie lo ignora) más propicia
   a la muerte.
¿Es posible que yo, súbdito de Yaqub Almansur,
Muera como tuvieron que morir las rosas y
   Aristóteles?

Del *Diván de Almotásim*
el Magrebí (siglo XII).

QUATRAIN

Others died, but that happened in the past,
Which is the season (no one doesn't know this) most
    propitious for death.
Is it possible that I, a subject of Yaqub Almansur,
Must die the way the roses and Aristotle had to die?

               From the *Diván de Almotásim*
                   el Magrebí (12th century)

                       [*Alan Dugan*]

LIMITES

Hay una línea de Verlaine que no volveré a recordar,
Hay una calle próxima que está vedada a mis pasos,
Hay un espejo que me ha visto por última vez,
Hay una puerta que he cerrado hasta el fin del mundo.
Entre los libros de mi biblioteca (estoy viéndolos)
Hay alguno que ya nunca abriré.
Este verano cumpliré cincuenta años:
La muerte me desgasta, incesante.

De *Inscripciones* (Montevideo, 1923)
de Julio Platero Haedo.

LIMITS (OR GOOD-BYES)

There's a line of Verlaine's that I'm not going to
    remember again.
There's a nearby street that's forbidden to my footsteps.
There's a mirror that has seen me for the last time.
There's a door I've closed until the end of the world.
Among the books in my library (I'm looking at them)
There are some I'll never open again.
This summer I'll be fifty years old:
Death invades me, constantly.

From *Inscripciones* by Julio Platero
Haedo (Montevideo, 1923)

[*Alan Dugan*]

EL POETA DECLARA SU NOMBRADIA

El círculo del cielo mide mi gloria,
Las bibliotecas del Oriente se disputan mis versos,
Los emires me buscan para llenarme de oro la boca,
Los ángeles ya saben de memoria mi último zéjel.
Mis instrumentos de trabajo son la humillación y la
    angustia;
Ojalá yo hubiera nacido muerto.

*Del Diván de Abulcasim
el Hadramí* (siglo XII).

THE POET TELLS OF HIS FAME

The rim of the sky is the measure of my glory,
The libraries of the East fight to own my verses,
The rulers seek me out to fill my mouth with gold,
The angels already know my last couplet by heart.
The tools of my art are humiliation and anguish.
Oh, if only I had been born dead!

From the *Diván de Abulcasim
el Hadramí* (12th century)

[*W. S. Merwin*]

EL ENEMIGO GENEROSO

*Magnus Barfod, en el año 1102, emprendió la con-
quista general de los reinos de Irlanda; se dice que la
víspera de su muerte recibió este saludo de Muirchertach, rey en Dublín:*

Que en tus ejércitos militen el oro y la tempestad,
    Magnus Barfod.
Que mañana, en los campos de mi reino, sea feliz
    tu batalla.
Que tus manos de rey tejan terribles la tela de la
    espada.
Que sean alimento del cisne rojo los que se oponen
    a tu espada.
Que te sacien de gloria tus muchos dioses, que te
    sacien de sangre.
Que seas victorioso en la aurora, rey que pisas a
    Irlanda.
Que de tus muchos días ninguno brille como el día
    de mañana.
Porque ese día será el último. Te lo juro, rey Magnus.
Porque antes que se borre su luz, te venceré y te
    borraré, Magnus Barfod.

Del *Anhang zur Heimskringla*
(1893) de H. Gering.

THE GENEROUS ENEMY

In the year 1102, Magnus Barfod undertook the general conquest of the Irish kingdoms; it is said that on the eve of his death he received this greeting from Muirchertach, the King of Dublin:

May gold and the storm fight on your side, Magnus
    Barfod.
May your fighting meet with good fortune, tomorrow,
    on the fields of my kingdom.
May your royal hands strike awe, weaving the sword's
    web.
May those who oppose your sword be food for the red
    swan.
May your many gods sate you with glory, may they sate
    you with blood.
May you be victorious in the dawn, King who tread
    upon Ireland.
May tomorrow shine the brightest of all your many days.
Because it will be your last. That I swear to you,
    King Magnus.
Because before its light is blotted out I will defeat you
    and blot you out, Magnus Barfod.

From the *Anhang zur Heimskringla*
by H. Gering (1893)

[*W. S. Merwin*]

Appendices

Notes

*Contents of the Principal Editions
of Borges' Poetry*

Index of Spanish and English Titles

I. NEW AND UNREPRINTED POEMS

Over the years and through successive editions of his collected poems, Borges has pruned many pieces. Recently he has even said—partly in truth, partly in exaggeration—that one reason he kept on writing poetry and adding it to new editions of his *Obra poética* was to have a pretext for leaving out certain poems he disliked. From the first collected edition, of 1943, to the latest, of 1969, nearly thirty poems have been suppressed. But these rejections are not only of work the author no longer feels any sympathy for; occasionally Borges will rewrite a poem and then, in a kind of substitution, drop the earlier version.

To illustrate what this unreprinted material is like, five rejected pieces are included here. "Blurred Dawn" and "Along the Byways of Nîmes" were never collected again after their appearances, respectively, in the first editions of *Fervor de Buenos Aires* and *Luna de enfrente*. The two poems on Colonel Francisco Borges and the one on Rafael Cansinos-Assens fall into the category of substitutions; "Carved on a Tombstone" was replaced in 1943 by "To Colonel Francisco Borges," which itself was dropped in 1967 after the author had taken up and perfected the same theme in "Allusion to the Death of Colonel Francisco Borges." These last three and the sonnet "Junín" should be compared. The poem to Cansinos, also left out of the 1967 edition, should be read with the more recent sonnet on him.

"The Southside" and "Rose," written in July or August, 1969, and quietly slipped into the latest revised edition of *Fervor de Buenos Aires,* are given a place here, since they have little in common either in tone or point of view with the early Borges.

The Spanish texts follow the translations and in each case were taken from the last printed version. In the second and fifth poems, slight modifications in accenting and typography have been made with the author's consent so as to conform both to his own styling and to the styling of this book; in the title of the fourth poem, the form of Cansinos' name has been corrected. For further details on the origins and histories of these and other unreprinted poems, see below, pp. 313–24.

BLURRED DAWN

The ships have gone blank
in the rectangular waters of the dock basin.
The cranes, at intervals, relax their tendons.
The masts are blunted in the shallow sky.
A choked siren vainly plucks
the strings of far-off spaces.
The ash of scattered good-byes
makes the whole place desolate,
and the passing gull
is a handkerchief that bids farewell,
its wingtips grazing
the axes of the prows that fell the forest of
    the seas.
Foreseen, miraculous,
the headlong dawn
will roll in from soul to soul.

[*Norman Thomas di Giovanni*]

CARVED ON A TOMBSTONE

For Colonel Francisco Borges,
my grandfather

The easy hills of Uruguay,
Paraguay's burning swamps
and the vanquished prairies
to your mind were
a single unending violence.
In the fighting at La Verde
death made inroads on so much bravery.
If for you this life turned out like steel
and your heart an angry mob
that thronged your breast,
may divine justice
enlist for you now all happiness
and may all immortality be with you.

[*Norman Thomas di Giovanni*]

TO COLONEL FRANCISCO BORGES (1833–1874)

For your life was this:
an object dragged from battle to battle.

Honor, poignancy, loneliness
and courage that served no end.

Montevideo and those killers in the pay of Oribe,
Uruguay's hogback ridges,
the fever-ridden swamps of Paraguay,
two Paraguayan bullets,
Jordán's mounted bands roaming the hill country,
the plains of Catriel and of Martín Fierro.

On the 26th of November 1874,
so that death might take you in its eye,
you wrapped yourself in a white poncho
and rode out on a silver-colored horse.

On the 28th of November 1874
you lay dying with two bullets in the stomach.

[*Norman Thomas di Giovanni*]

TO RAFAEL CANSINOS-ASSENS

Long and final passage over the breathtaking height
    of the trestle's span.
At our feet the wind gropes for sails
and the stars throb intensity.
We relish the taste of the night, transfixed by
    darkness—night become now again a habit of
    our flesh.
The final night of our talking
before the sea-miles part us.
Still ours is the silence
where like meadows the voices glitter.
Dawn is still a bird lost
in the most distant vileness of the world.
This last night of all, sheltered
from the great wind of absence.
The inwardness of Good-bye is tragic
like that of every event in which Time is manifest.
It is bitter to realize that we shall not even have
the stars in common.
When evening is quietness in my patio,
from your pages morning will rise.
Your winter will be the shadow of my summer
and your light the glory of my shadow.
Still we persist together.
Still our two voices achieve understanding
like the intensity and tenderness of sundown.

[*Robert Fitzgerald*]

ALONG THE BYWAYS OF NIMES

Like those roads back home
which stand out in my memory,
this tree-lined way in Provence
draws its simple Roman straightness
through Nîmes' broad suburbs
full of space and a generosity of plain.
The water intones in a ditch
the sorrow that suits its restless journey,
and its murmuring is a first awakening,
and night comes on kindly as a tree,
and the loneliness urges me along on my walk.
This place is much like happiness,
yet I myself am not happy.
The sky is living out a full moon,
and from a doorway a music reaches me
that dies in love
and with pained relief comes back.
My own dark worries mortify the calm.
I am deeply wrought
by the shame of being sad among so much beauty
and the disgrace of unfulfilled hopes.

[*Norman Thomas di Giovanni*]

THE SOUTHSIDE

From one of your patios to have looked up
at the ancient stars,   '
from a bench in deep shadow to have looked up
at those scattered points of light,
which my ignorance never learned to name
or to order into constellations,
to have been aware of the circle of water
in the hidden cistern,
of the odor of jasmine and honeysuckle,
the silence of the bird asleep,

the arch of the entranceway, the damp—
these things, perhaps, are the poem.

[*Norman Thomas di Giovanni*]

ROSE

Rose,
the unfading rose beyond my verse—
rose that's full and fragrant,
rose of the black garden in the deep of night,
rose of any garden and any night,
rose that's born again by the art of alchemy
out of tenuous ash,
rose of the Persians and Ariosto,
rose that's always by itself,
rose that's always the rose of roses,
the young Platonic flower,
the blind and burning rose beyond my verse,
unattainable rose.

[*Norman Thomas di Giovanni*]

ALBA DESDIBUJADA

Se apagaron los barcos
en el agua cuadrada de la dársena.
Las periódicas grúas relajan sus tendones.
Los mástiles se embotan en el cielo playo.
Una sirena ahogada pulsa en vano
las cuerdas de la distancia.
La ceniza de adioses aventados
va agostando el paraje
y es un pañuelo en despedida
la gaviota que pasa
rozando con las alas
las hachas de las proas que talan la foresta
    de los mares.

En previsto milagro
la aurora despeñada
rodará de alma en alma.

INSCRIPCION SEPULCRAL

*Para el coronel Francisco
Borges, mi abuelo*

Las cariñosas lomas orientales,
los ardientes esteros paraguayos
y la pampa rendida
fueron ante tu alma
una sola violencia continuada.
En el combate de La Verde
desbarató tanto valor la muerte.
Si esta vida contigo fue acerada
y el corazón, airada muchedumbre
se te agolpó en el pecho,
ruego al justo destino
aliste para tí toda la dicha
y que toda la inmortalidad sea contigo.

AL CORONEL FRANCISCO BORGES
(*1833–1874*)

Porque eso fue tu vida:
Una cosa que arrastran las batallas.

El honor, la tristeza, la soledad
y el inútil coraje.

Montevideo y los mazorqueros de Oribe,
las resueltas cuchillas orientales,
los febriles esteros del Paraguay,
dos balas paraguayas,
la montonera jordanista en los montes,
la pampa de Catriel y de Martín Fierro.

El día 26 de noviembre de 1874,
para que te viera la muerte,
montabas un caballo plateado
y te envolviste en un poncho blanco.

El día 28 de noviembre de 1874,
morías con dos balas en el estómago.

A RAFAEL CANSINOS-ASSENS

Larga y final andanza sobre la arrebatada
    exaltación del ala del viaducto.
El viento, a nuestros pies, busca velámenes,
y las estrellas laten intensidad.
Bien paladeado el gusto de la noche, traspasados
    de sombra, vuelta ya una costumbre de nuestra
    carne la noche.
Noche postrer de nuestro diálogo,
antes de que nos separen las leguas.
Aun es nuestro el silencio
donde como praderas resplandecen las voces.
Aun el alba es un pájaro perdido
en la vileza más remota del mundo.
Ultima noche resguardada
del gran viento de ausencia.
Es trágica la entraña del adiós
como de todo acontecer en que es notorio el
    Tiempo.
Es duro realizar que ni tendremos
en común las estrellas.
Cuando la tarde sea quietud en mi patio,
de tus carillas surgirá la mañana.
Será la sombra de mi verano tu invierno
y tu luz será gloria de mi sombra.
Aun persistimos juntos.
Aun las dos voces logran convivir,
como la intensidad y la ternura en las puestas
    de sol.

POR LOS VIALES DE NIMES

Como esas calles patrias
cuya firmeza en mi recordación es reclamo
esta alameda provenzal
tiende su fácil rectitud latina
por un ancho suburbio
donde hay despejo y generosidad de llanura.
El agua va rezando por una acequia
el dolor que conviene a su peregrinación insentida
y la susurración es ensayo de alma
y la noche es benigna como un árbol
y la soledad persuade a la andanza.
Este lugar es semejante a la dicha;
y yo no soy feliz.
El cielo está viviendo un plenilunio
y un portalejo me declara una música
que en el amor se muere
y con alivio dolorido resurge.
Mi oscuridad difícil mortifica la calma.
Tenaces me suscitan
la afrenta de estar triste en la hermosura
y el deshonor de insatisfecha esperanza.

EL SUR

Desde uno de tus patios haber mirado
las antiguas estrellas,
desde el banco de la sombra haber mirado
esas luces dispersas
que mi ignorancia no ha aprendido a nombrar
ni a ordenar en constelaciones,
haber sentido el círculo del agua
en el secreto aljibe,
el olor del jazmín y la madreselva,
el silencio del pájaro dormido,
el arco del zaguán, la humedad
—esas cosas, acaso, son el poema.

LA ROSA

La rosa,
la inmarcesible rosa que no canto,
la que es peso y fragancia,
la del negro jardín en la alta noche,
la de cualquier jardín y cualquier tarde,
la rosa que resurge de la tenue
ceniza por el arte de la alquimia,
la rosa de los persas y de Ariosto,
la que siempre está sola,
la que siempre es la rosa de las rosas,
la joven flor platónica,
la ardiente y ciega rosa que no canto,
la rosa inalcanzable.

II. PROSE PIECES FROM EL HACEDOR

One of the celebrated aspects of Borges' style has been his frequent blurring or abolishment of the boundaries between the short story and essay forms. "The Approach to al-Mu'tasim" is read as a review in one of his books and as a story in another, and among the miniature essays of *The Book of Imaginary Beings* are a number of wholly made-up pieces. Similarly, Borges draws no great distinction between his poems and a number of his short prose pieces, often disclaiming any essential difference between poetry and prose at all and saying he writes the one or the other merely to suit private needs or moods. "The Dagger," printed in this volume as a poem, appears with only minor typographical modifications as Chapter IX in his book on Evaristo Carriego. Twice— in *El hacedor* (The Maker) and in *Elogio de la sombra* (In Praise of Darkness)—Borges has collected poems and short prose works together. In this light, five pieces from *El hacedor* have been chosen for inclusion here. These poems in prose were all written in the late 1950's. The original texts are printed following the English versions.

THE MAKER

Until then, he had never dwelled on the pleasures of memory. Impressions had always washed over him, fleeting and vivid. A potter's design in vermilion; the vault of heaven clustered with stars that were also gods; the moon, from which a lion had fallen; the smoothness of marble under one's lingering fingertips; the taste of boar meat, which he liked to strip with quick flashing bites; a Phoenician word; the black shadow cast by a spear on yellow sand; the nearness of the sea or of women; the heavy wine whose roughness he cut with honey—any of these could wholly encompass the range of his mind. He was acquainted with fear as well as with anger and courage, and once he was the first to scale an enemy wall. Eager, curious, unquestioning, following no other law than to enjoy things and forget them, he wandered over many lands and, on one side or the other of the sea, looked on the cities of men and their palaces. In bustling marketplaces or at the foot of a mountain whose hidden peak may have sheltered satyrs, he had heard entangled stories, which he accepted as he accepted reality, without attempting to find out whether they were true or imaginary.

Little by little, the beautiful world began to leave him; a persistent mist erased the lines of his hand, the night lost its multitude of stars, the ground became uncertain beneath his steps. Everything grew distant and blurred. When he knew he was going blind, he cried out; stoic fortitude had not yet been invented, and Hector could flee from Achilles without dishonor. I shall no longer look upon the sky and its mythological dread (he felt), nor this face which the years will transform. Days and nights passed over these fears of his body, but one morning he awoke, looked (without astonishment now) at the dim things around him, and unexplainably felt—the way one recognizes a strain of music or a voice—that all this had already happened to him and that he had faced it with fear, but also with joy, hope, and curiosity. Then he went deep into his past, which seemed to him bottomless, and managed to draw out of that dizzying descent the lost memory that now shone like a coin under the rain, maybe because he had never recalled it before except in some dream.

This was the memory. Another boy had wronged him and he had gone to his father and told him the story. His father, letting him speak, appeared not to listen or understand, and took down from the wall a bronze dagger, beautiful and charged with power, which in secret the boy had coveted. Now it lay in his hands and the suddenness of possession wiped out the injury he had suffered, but his father's voice was telling him, "Let them know you're a man," and in that voice was a command. Night blinded the paths. Clasping the dagger, in which he felt a magic power, he scrambled down the steep hillside that surrounded the house and ran to the edge of the sea, thinking of himself as Ajax and Perseus and peopling with wounds and battles the dark salt air. The exact taste of that moment was what he now sought. The rest mattered little to him—the insults leading to the challenge, the clumsy fight, the way home with the blade dripping blood.

Another memory, also involving night and an expectation of adventure, sprang out of that one. A woman, the first to be given him by the gods, had waited for him in the shadow of a crypt until he reached her through galleries that were like nets of stone and down slopes that sank into darkness. Why did these memories come back to him and why without bitterness, as if foretelling of things about to happen?

With slow amazement he understood. In this nighttime of his mortal eyes into which he was now descending, love and danger were also in wait for him—Ares and Aphrodite—because he already divined (because he was already ringed in by) a rumor of hexameters and glory, a rumor of men defending a shrine which the gods would not save and of black ships roaming the seas in search of a loved island, the rumor of the Odysseys and the Iliads it was his destiny to sing and to leave resounding forever in mankind's hollow memory. These things we know, but not what he felt when he went down into his final darkness.

A YELLOW ROSE

It happened neither on that afternoon nor on the next, but when the renowned Giambattista Marino died—the man whom the many mouths of Fame (to use an image that was dear to him) proclaimed the new Homer and the new Dante—the silent inner event that had occurred was, essentially, the last of his life. Burdened with years and glory, the man lay dying in a broad Spanish bed with tall carved corner posts. It is easy to picture a quiet balcony a few steps away, looking toward the sunset, and farther below marble statuary and laurel trees and a garden whose terraces are reflected in a rectangle of water. A woman has placed a yellow rose in a vase; the man murmurs the inevitable verses of which he himself, to speak truthfully, is rather weary:

> *Deep purple of the garden, pride of the lawn,*
> *Springtime's jewel, fair April's eye . . .*

Then the revelation came to him. Marino *saw* the rose as Adam first saw it in Paradise, and he felt that it lived in an eternity of its own and not in his words, and that we may mention or allude to a thing but not express it, and that the tall proud volumes casting a golden haze there in a corner of the room were not (as his vanity dreamed) a mirror of the world, but only one thing more added to the world.

This illumination came to Marino on the eve of his death, as perhaps before him it had come to Homer and to Dante as well.

THE WITNESS

In a stable nearly in the shadow of the new stone church, a gray-eyed, gray-bearded cowherd lies amid the stench of cattle and quietly seeks death the way a man seeks sleep. Obedient to vast secret laws, the lights and shadows of the day play on the rough walls of the hovel. Close by are tilled fields and a dry ditch clogged with dead leaves, and in the black soil at the edge of the woods the tracks of a wolf. The man sleeps and dreams, forgotten. The bells for evening prayer awaken him. By now the sound of bells is one of evening's customs in the kingdoms of England, but as a child the man had known the face of Woden, the holy awe and loud exultation of his worship, the clumsy wooden idol laden with Roman coins and coarse vestments, and the sacrifice of horses, dogs, and prisoners. Before daybreak he will die, and with him will die—never to come back again—the last actual images of heathen rites. When this Saxon is gone, the world will be a little poorer.

Events that fill up space and reach their end when someone dies may cause us wonder, but some thing—or an endless number of things—dies with each man's last breath, unless, as theosophy conjectures, the world has a memory. In the past, there was a day when the last eyes to have seen Christ were closed; the battle of Junín and Helen's face each died with the death of some one man. What will die with me when I die, what pathetic or worthless memory will be lost to the world? The voice of Macedonio Fernández, the image of a brown horse grazing in an empty lot at the corner of Serrano and Charcas, a stick of sulphur in the drawer of a mahogany desk?

EVERYTHING AND NOTHING

In him there was no one. Behind his face (even in the poor paintings of the period it is unlike any other) and his words (which were swarming, fanciful, and excited), there was only a touch of coldness, a dream undreamed by anyone. At first he thought all people were like him, but when he had tried to explain this inner emptiness, a schoolmate's blank look showed him his mistake and made him realize from then on that an individual had best not differ from his species. From time to time he thought books might cure this strange ailment, and in this way he learned the small Latin and less Greek of which a contemporary was to remark. Later on he considered that in the practice of one of humanity's age-old habits he might actually find what he was looking for, and during the course of a long, lazy June afternoon he let himself be initiated by Anne Hathaway. In his twenties he went to London. By instinct, so as to cover up the fact that he was nobody, he had grown skilled in the trick of making believe he was somebody. There in London he came to the profession to which he was destined—that of the actor, who on a stage plays at being someone else before an audience who plays at taking him for that other person. Stagecraft brought him singular happiness, perhaps the first he ever knew, but once the last line was spoken and the last corpse carted off, a hateful taste of the unreal came down on him. He was no longer Ferrex or Tamburlaine and went back to being nobody. So driven, he began to imagine other heroes and other tragic tales. And while in London bawdyhouses and taverns his flesh fulfilled its destiny as flesh, the spirit that inhabited him was Caesar, ignoring the augur's prophecy, and Juliet, hating the lark, and Macbeth, speaking on the heath to the witches, who are also the Fates. No one was ever so many men as this man, who, like the Egyptian Proteus, could run through all of life's guises. Occasionally, he left a confession in some nook of his work, sure it would never be deciphered; Richard II says that in one person he plays many people, and with strange words Iago says, "I am not what I am." The underlying sameness of existing, dreaming, and acting inspired him to famous pages.

For twenty years he persisted in this willful hallucination, but one day he was overcome by the surfeit and the horror of being so many kings who die by the sword and so many star-crossed lovers who meet and who part and who at last so melodiously die. That same day he decided to sell his theater. Before a week was over, he had gone back to the village of his birth, where again he discovered the trees and the river of his childhood, never linking them to those other trees and rivers—made illustrious by mythological allusions and Latin words—which his muse had celebrated. He had to be someone; he became a retired stage manager who has made his fortune and to whom loans, lawsuits, and petty usury are amusements. In this personage, he dictated the dry testament that has come down to us, in which he deliberately avoided any trace of the pathetic or the literary. Friends from London used to visit him in his country retreat, and for their sake he again took up the part of poet.

The tale runs that before or after death, when he stood face to face with God, he said to Him, "I, who in vain have been so many men, want to be one man—myself." The voice of the Lord answered him out of the whirlwind, "I too have no self; I dreamed the world as you dreamed your work, my Shakespeare, and among the shapes of my dream are you, who, like me, are many men and no one."

BORGES AND MYSELF

It's to the other man, to Borges, that things happen. I walk along the streets of Buenos Aires, stopping now and then—perhaps out of habit—to look at the arch of an old entranceway or a grillwork gate; of Borges I get news through the mail and glimpse his name among a committee of professors or in a dictionary of biography. I have a taste for hourglasses, maps, eighteenth-century typography, the roots of words, the smell of coffee, and Stevenson's prose; the other man shares these likes, but in a showy way that turns them into stagy mannerisms. It would be an exaggeration to say that we are on bad terms; I live, I let myself live, so that Borges can weave his tales and poems, and those tales and poems are my justification. It is not hard for me to admit that he has managed to write a few worthwhile pages, but these pages cannot save me, perhaps because what is good no longer belongs to any-one—not even the other man—but rather to speech or tradition. In any case, I am fated to become lost once and for all, and only some moment of myself will survive in the other man. Little by little, I have been surrendering everything to him, even though I have evidence of his stubborn habit of falsification and exaggerating. Spinoza held that all things try to keep on being themselves; a stone wants to be a stone and the tiger a tiger. I shall remain in Borges, not in myself (if it is so that I am someone), but I recognize myself less in his books than in those of others or than in the laborious tuning of a guitar. Years ago, I tried ridding myself of him, and I went from myths of the outlying slums of the city to games with time and infinity, but those games are now part of Borges, and I will have to turn to other things. And so, my life is a running away, and I lose everything and everything is left to oblivion or to the other man.

Which of us is writing this page I don't know.

[Translations by Norman Thomas di Giovanni
in collaboration with the author]

EL HACEDOR

Nunca se había demorado en los goces de la memoria. Las impresiones resbalaban sobre él, momentáneas y vívidas; el bermellón de un alfarero, la bóveda cargada de estrellas que también eran dioses, la luna, de la que había caído un león, la lisura del mármol bajo las lentas yemas sensibles, el sabor de la carne de jabalí, que le gustaba desgarrar con dentelladas blancas y bruscas, una palabra fenicia, la sombra negra que una lanza proyecta en la arena amarilla, la cercanía del mar o de las mujeres, el pesado vino cuya aspereza mitigaba la miel, podían abarcar por entero el ámbito de su alma.

Conocía el terror pero también la cólera y el coraje, y una vez fue el primero en escalar un muro enemigo. Ávido, curioso, casual, sin otra ley que la fruición y la indiferencia inmediata, anduvo por la variada tierra y miró, en una u otra margen del mar, las ciudades de los hombres y sus palacios. En los mercados populosos o al pie de una montaña de cumbre incierta, en la que bien podía haber sátiros, había escuchado complicadas historias, que recibió como recibía la realidad, sin indagar si eran verdaderas o falsas.

Gradualmente, el hermoso universo fue abandonándolo; una terca neblina le borró las líneas de la mano, la noche se despobló de estrellas, la tierra era insegura bajo sus pies. Todo se alejaba y se confundía. Cuando supo que se estaba quedando ciego, gritó; el pudor estoico no había sido aún inventado y Héctor podía huir sin desmedro. *Ya no veré* (sintió) *ni el cielo lleno de pavor mitológico, ni esta cara que los años transformarán.* Días y noches pasaron sobre esa desesperación de su carne, pero una mañana se despertó, miró (ya sin asombro) las borrosas cosas que lo rodeaban e inexplicablemente sintió, como quien reconoce una música o una voz, que ya le había ocurrido todo eso y que lo había encarado con temor, pero también con júbilo, esperanza y curiosidad. Entonces descendió a su memoria, que le pareció interminable, y logró sacar de aquel vértigo el recuerdo perdido que relució como una moneda bajo la lluvia, acaso porque nunca lo había mirado, salvo, quizá, en un sueño.

El recuerdo era así. Lo había injuriado otro muchacho y él había acudido a su padre y le había contado la historia. Este lo dejó hablar como si no escuchara o no comprendiera y descolgó de la pared un puñal de bronce, bello y cargado de poder, que el chico había codiciado furtivamente. Ahora lo tenía en las manos y la sorpresa de la posesión anuló la injuria padecida, pero la voz del padre estaba diciendo: *Que alguien sepa que eres un hombre,* y había una orden en la voz. La noche cegaba los caminos; abrazado al puñal, en el que presentía una fuerza mágica, descendió la brusca ladera que rodeaba la casa y corrió a la orilla del mar, soñándose Ayax y Perseo y poblando de heridas y de batallas la oscuridad salobre. El sabor preciso de aquel momento era lo que ahora buscaba; no le importaba lo demás: las afrentas del desafío, el torpe combate, el regreso con la hoja sangrienta.

Otro recuerdo, en el que también había una noche y una inminencia de aventura, brotó de aquél. Una mujer, la primera que le depararon los dioses, lo había esperado en la sombra de un hipogeo, y él la buscó por galerías que eran como redes de piedra y por declives que se hundían en la sombra. ¿Por qué le llegaban esas memorias y por qué le llegaban sin amargura, como una mera prefiguración del presente?

Con grave asombro comprendió. En esta noche de sus ojos mortales, a la que ahora descendía, lo aguardaban también el amor y el riesgo. Ares y Afrodita, porque ya adivinaba (porque ya lo cercaba) un rumor de gloria y de hexámetros, un rumor de hombres que defienden un templo que los dioses no salvarán y de bajeles negros que buscan por el mar una isla querida, el rumor de las Odiseas e Ilíadas que era su destino cantar y dejar resonando cóncavamente en la memoria humana. Sabemos estas cosas, pero no las que sintió al descender a la última sombra.

UNA ROSA AMARILLA

Ni aquella tarde ni la otra murió el ilustre Giambattista Marino, que las bocas unánimes de la Fama (para usar una imagen que le fue cara) proclamaron el nuevo Homero y el nuevo Dante, pero el hecho inmóvil y silencioso que entonces ocurrió fue en verdad el último de su vida. Colmado de años y de gloria, el hombre se moría en un vasto lecho español de columnas labradas. Nada cuesta imaginar a unos pasos un sereno balcón que mira al poniente y, más abajo, mármoles y laureles y un jardín que duplica sus graderías en un agua rectangular. Una mujer ha puesto en una copa una rosa amarilla; el hombre murmura los versos inevitables que a él mismo, para hablar con sinceridad, ya lo hastían un poco:

Púrpura del jardín, pompa del prado,
gema de primavera, ojo de abril . . .

Entonces ocurrió la revelación. Marino *vio* la rosa, como Adán pudo verla en el Paraíso, y sintió que ella estaba en su eternidad y no en sus palabras y que podemos mencionar o aludir pero no expresar y que los altos y soberbios volúmenes que formaban en un ángulo de la sala una penumbra de oro no eran (como su vanidad soñó) un espejo del mundo, sino una cosa más agregada al mundo.

Esta iluminación alcanzó Marino en la víspera de su muerte, y Homero y Dante acaso la alcanzaron también.

EL TESTIGO

En un establo que está casi a la sombra de la nueva iglesia de piedra, un hombre de ojos grises y barba gris, tendido entre el olor de los animales, humildemente busca la muerte como quien busca el sueño. El día, fiel a vastas leyes secretas, va desplazando y confundiendo las sombras en el pobre recinto; afuera están las tierras aradas y un zanjón cegado por hojas muertas y algún rastro de lobo en el barro negro donde empiezan los bosques. El hombre duerme y sueña, olvidado. El toque de oración lo despierta. En los reinos de Inglaterra el son de campanas ya es uno de los hábitos de la tarde, pero el hombre, de niño, ha visto la cara de Woden, el horror divino y la exultación, el torpe ídolo de madera recargado de monedas romanas y de vestiduras pesadas, el sacrificio de caballos, perros y prisioneros. Antes del alba morirá y con él morirán, y no volverán, las últimas imágenes inmediatas de los ritos paganos; el mundo será un poco más pobre cuando este sajón haya muerto.

Hechos que pueblan el espacio y que tocan a su fin cuando alguien se muere pueden maravillarnos, pero una cosa, o un número infinito de cosas, muere en cada agonía, salvo que exista una memoria del universo, como han conjeturado los teósofos. En el tiempo hubo un día que apagó los últimos ojos que vieron a Cristo; la batalla de Junín y el amor de Helena murieron con la muerte de un hombre. ¿Qué morirá conmigo cuando yo muera, qué forma patética o deleznable perderá el mundo? ¿La voz de Macedonio Fernández, la imagen de un caballo colorado en el baldío de Serrano y de Charcas, una barra de azufre en el cajón de un escritorio de caoba?

EVERYTHING AND NOTHING

Nadie hubo en él; detrás de su rostro (que aun a través de las malas pinturas de la época no se parece a ningún otro) y de sus palabras, que eran copiosas, fantásticas y agitadas, no había más que un poco de frío, un sueño no soñado por alguien. Al principio creyó que todas las personas eran como él, pero la extrañeza de un compañero con el que había empezado a comentar esa vacuidad le reveló su error y le dejó sentir, para siempre, que un individuo no debe diferir de la especie. Alguna vez pensó que en los libros hallaría remedio para su mal y así aprendió el poco latín y menos griego de que hablaría un contemporáneo; después consideró que en el ejercicio de un rito elemental de la humanidad, bien podía estar lo que buscaba y se dejó iniciar por Anne Hathaway, durante una larga siesta de junio. A los veintitantos años fue a Londres. Instintivamente, ya se había adiestrado en el hábito de simular que era alguien, para que no se descubriera su condición de nadie; en Londres encontró la profesión a la que estaba predestinado, la del actor, que en un escenario, juega a ser otro, ante un concurso de personas que juegan a tomarlo por aquel otro. Las tareas histriónicas le enseñaron una felicidad singular, acaso la primera que conoció; pero aclamado el último verso y retirado de la escena el último muerto, el odiado sabor de la irrealidad recaía sobre él. Dejaba de ser Ferrex o Tamerlán y volvía a ser nadie. Acosado, dio en imaginar otros héroes y otras fábulas trágicas. Así, mientras el cuerpo cumplía su destino de cuerpo, en lupanares y tabernas de Londres, el alma que lo habitaba era César, que desoye la admonición del augur, y Julieta, que aborrece a la alondra, y Macbeth, que conversa en el páramo con las brujas que también son las parcas. Nadie fue tantos hombres como aquel hombre, que a semejanza del egipcio Proteo pudo agotar todas las apariencias del ser. A veces, dejó en algún recodo de la obra una confesión, seguro de que no la descifrarían; Ricardo afirma que en su sola persona, hace el papel de muchos, y Yago dice con curiosas palabras *no soy lo que soy*. La identidad fundamental de existir, soñar y representar le inspiró pasajes famosos.

Veinte años persistió en esa alucinación dirigida, pero una mañana lo sobrecogieron el hastío y el horror de ser tantos reyes que mueren por la espada y tantos desdichados amantes que convergen, divergen y melodiosamente agonizan. Aquel mismo día resolvió la venta de su teatro. Antes de una semana había regresado al pueblo natal, donde recuperó los árboles y el río de la niñez y no los vinculó a aquellos otros que había celebrado su musa, ilustres de alusión mitológica y de voces latinas. Tenía que ser alguien; fue un empresario retirado que ha hecho fortuna y a quien le interesan los préstamos, los litigios y la pequeña usura. En ese carácter dictó el árido testamento que conocemos, del que deliberadamente excluyó todo rasgo patético o literario. Solían visitar su retiro amigos de Londres, y él retomaba para ellos el papel de poeta.

La historia agrega que, antes o después de morir, se supo frente a Dios y le dijo: *Yo, que tantos hombres he sido en vano, quiero ser uno y yo.* La voz de Dios le contestó desde un torbellino: *Yo tam-*

poco soy; yo soñé el mundo como tú soñaste tu obra, mi Shake-
speare, y entre las formas de mi sueño estás tú, que como yo eres
muchos y nadie.

BORGES Y YO

Al otro, a Borges, es a quien le ocurren las cosas. Yo camino por
Buenos Aires y me demoro, acaso ya mecánicamente, para mirar
el arco de un zaguán y la puerta cancel; de Borges tengo noticias
por el correo y veo su nombre en una terna de profesores o en un
diccionario biográfico. Me gustan los relojes de arena, los mapas, la
tipografía del siglo XVIII, las etimologías, el sabor del café y la prosa
de Stevenson; el otro comparte esas preferencias, pero de un modo
vanidoso que las convierte en atributos de un actor. Sería exagerado
afirmar que nuestra relación es hostil; yo vivo, yo me dejo vivir, para
que Borges pueda tramar su literatura y esa literatura me justifica.
Nada me cuesta confesar que ha logrado ciertas páginas válidas,
pero esas páginas no me pueden salvar, quizá porque lo bueno ya
no es de nadie, ni siquiera del otro, sino del lenguaje o la tradición.
Por lo demás, yo estoy destinado a perderme, definitivamente, y sólo
algún instante de mí podrá sobrevivir en el otro. Poco a poco voy
cediéndole todo, aunque me consta su perversa costumbre de falsear
y magnificar. Spinoza entendió que todas las cosas quieren perse-
verar en su ser; la piedra eternamente quiere ser piedra y el tigre un
tigre. Yo he de quedar en Borges, no en mí (si es que alguien soy),
pero me reconozco menos en sus libros que en muchos otros o que
en el laborioso rasgueo de una guitarra. Hace años yo traté de
librarme de él y pasé de las mitologías del arrabal a los juegos con el
tiempo y con lo infinito, pero esos juegos son de Borges ahora y
tendré que idear otras cosas. Así mi vida es una fuga y todo lo
pierdo y todo es del olvido, o del otro.
No sé cuál de los dos escribe esta página.

III. PREFACES AND A DEDICATION

As a writer of forewords to his own and to other people's books, Borges has been prolific. In the case of the prefaces to his poetry, they are his only direct written comment on that body of his work. Informal, highly personal, always readable, they are often invaluable for their hints and insights.

There are nine prefaces to the fifteen principal volumes of Borges' poetry. All but one of these are presented here (the preface to *Elogio de la sombra* [In Praise of Darkness] will appear in the translation of that book in 1973), together with two informative prefaces to work in the sonnet form and to poems on northern themes, which have appeared only in small, privately printed editions.

The forewords to the first two collections of poems were understandably never reprinted. They were composed in a tortuous, seventeenth-century kind of prose that we have made no attempt to imitate in English. In fact, Borges, in a particularly indulgent mood when he allowed these English versions to be made, wanted it clear that we were not really translating the pieces but explaining them. I quote the original opening sentence of the first preface to indicate what is meant by this:

Suelen ser las prefaciones de autor una componenda mal pergeñada, entre la primordial jactancia de quien ampara obra que es propiamente facción suya, y la humildad que aconsejan la mundología y el uso.

A recent dedicatory piece is also included in this section.

[Preface to the 1923 edition of *Fervor de Buenos Aires*]

TO THE READER

Authors' prefaces are usually a halfway compromise between the arrogance of someone defending his own work and the modesty demanded by established tradition. This foreword will hold to that custom.

I shall start out by observing that my poems, in spite of the misleading suggestion of their title, are not—nor did they for a single moment ever attempt to be—a compendium of the many aspects and places of my city. In this volume, Buenos Aires does not stand for the topographical convention implied by its name; it is my home, its familiar neighborhoods, and, along with them, what I experienced of love, of suffering, and of misgivings.

On purpose, then, I have left out what I feel to be foreign to Buenos Aires: the rush of certain downtown streets, and the sad and common mobs that are found in any port—elements which have little to do with the laziness of a South American town. Without looking forward to what may come, nor wistful for the past, my poetry tries to represent present-day Buenos Aires, the amazement and the wonder of the places my long rambles lead me. Akin to the Romans, who would murmur the words *"numen inest"* on passing through a woods, "here dwells a god" my verses declare, stating the wonder of the streets deified by hope or by memory. Everyday places become, little by little, holy.

I realize that such intentions will sound strange to these times, whose poetry usually melts into mere word-music or descends to a pack of showy trifles. I speak without condemnation, but I consider myself justified. One cannot help disliking the writer who piles words on words, unsure of their inner marvels, or the writer who tries to make his work glitter by the mention of gold and jewels, thereby shaming with so much illumination our own rather drab verses, which take their light only from the modest glow of sunsets at the end of the street. To the decoratively visual and shining lyric bequeathed us by Góngora through his heir

Rubén Darío, I have tried to set up another—thoughtful, built up of intellectual adventures, and whose articles of faith may be summed up in the following words from Sir Thomas Browne (*Religio Medici,* 1643):

> Now for my life, it is a miracle, which to relate, were not a History, but a piece of Poetry, and would sound to common ears like a Fable. There is surely a piece of Divinity in us, something that was before the Elements, and owes no homage unto the Sun. He that understands not thus much is yet to begin the Alphabet of man.*

As to the form—rather than the essence—of my verses, it was my aim to pattern them after Heine's *The North Sea.* There are, however, some formal differences. The plainness and certainty of Spanish pronunciation, with its abundance of open vowels, do not permit the language to be made into absolutely free verse and therefore demand the use of assonances. The eleven-syllable line is now so natural to us that I have abounded in verses of that measure.

About the language I have little to say. I have always tried to use words—I cannot say whether successfully or not—according to their root meanings, a much more difficult task than supposed by writers who, without achieving new images, fall into a lazy and careless style. Only certain words afford me sensual pleasure, a defect found in all writers I know and whose one exception was Quevedo, who wallowed in the fullness of the Spanish tongue.

I have always been fond of coining metaphors, but at the same time I always put effectiveness before mere novelty. In this book there are several pieces made by stringing out metaphors, a method which reached perfection in short poems by Jacobo Sureda, J. Rivas-Panedas, and Norah Lange, but which of course is not the only one. This statement—which must seem obvious to the reader—will be blasphemous to many sectarian comrades.

If in the following pages there is some successful verse or other, may the reader forgive me the audacity of having written it before him. We are all one; our inconsequential minds are much alike, and circumstances so influence us that it is something of an accident that you are the reader and I the writer—the unsure, ardent writer—of my verses.†

J.L.B.

* Part II, section 11. For the sake of readability, Borges' custom of not indicating ellipses in quoted matter is followed here. *Ed.*
† In all subsequent editions of *Fervor de Buenos Aires,* Borges has reprinted—in a briefer, revised form—only the concluding paragraph of this preface. It is translated as follows in its current (since 1958) wording; in the 1943 and 1954 editions

[Preface to the 1925 edition of *Luna de enfrente*]

TO THE POSSIBLE READER

This book is a token of my poverty, written not in passion but in meditation. In these pages the reader will find a long, weary street out in the western stretches of town, sad in the sunset, and the loneliness of love denied. Our daily lives are a dialogue between life and death, woven of memories (shapes of having been and being no longer) or else of plans: mere hope of being. A great deal of non-life is in us, and chess, gatherings, lectures, small tasks are at times but appearances of life, ways of being dead. Let every poet praise the things that are akin to himself, for that is really poetry. I have celebrated those things akin to me, those things I deeply feel. They are the blue walls of the city's outlying slums and the tiny squares brimming with sky. This is all I have; here I offer it to you.

I am in no mood for the discussion of technique. The music of verse hardly interests me, so that I find all of its forms suitable as long as rhyme is unobtrusive. Many of the pieces in this book attempt our Argentine speech, not in jargon of the plains or of the city's tenements but in the diverse, everyday talk of Buenos Aires. Others attempt that timeless, abstract Spanish (neither from Castile nor from South America) which is found in any dictionary. In two of them figure the name of Evaristo Carriego, always as something of a minor deity of Palermo, for that is how I feel him. But another far more overwhelming shadow than his is cast over the neighborhood—that of Juan Manuel de Rosas.

I want to explain the title, if need be. *Moon Across the Way*. The moon (the moon that walks in brightness, I recently read in Fray Luis de León) is in itself a symbol of poetry. The across the way does not change this but makes it into a city moon, brings it nearer, turning it into a Buenos Aires moon, everyone's moon. This is the way I like it, and this is the way I see it from the street.

J.L.B.

---

of the *Poemas*, in the first line, "offer" had read "admit": *If the pages of this book offer some felicitous line or other, may the reader pardon me the discourtesy of having claimed it first. Our inconsequential selves differ but little; the circumstance that you are the reader and I the writer of these exercises is accidental and irrelevant. Ed.*

[Preface to *El hacedor* (1960); to the "El otro, el mismo" section of the 1964, 1966, and 1967 editions of *Obra poética;* and a second preface to *El otro, el mismo* (1969)]

TO LEOPOLDO LUGONES

Leaving behind the sounds of the plaza, I enter the Library. At once, in an almost physical way, I feel the gravitation of the books, the quiet atmosphere of ordered things, the past rescued and magically preserved. To left and right, rapt in lucid dream, the momentary profiles of the readers' faces are outlined by the light (as in Milton's hypallage) of their studious lamps. I recall having recalled this figure before, in this same place, and then that other epithet also defined by what surrounds it, "the arid camel" of your *Lunario sentimental,* and afterward that hexameter from Virgil which employs the same device and goes beyond it:

Ibant obscuri sola sub nocte per umbram.

These reminiscences lead me to the door of your office. I enter. We exchange a few conventional and cordial words, and I hand you this book. If I am not mistaken, you were rather fond of me, Lugones, and it would have pleased you to be pleased by some work of mine. That never happened, but this time you turn the pages and read approvingly some line or other, maybe because you recognize your own voice in it, maybe because my faulty execution means less to you than the soundness of my aims.

At this point my dream dissolves—like water in water. The vast library all around me is on Mexico Street, not on Rodríguez Peña, and you, Lugones, committed suicide around the beginning of 1938. My vanity and my wistfulness have set up an impossible scene. This may be so (I tell myself), but tomorrow I too will be dead and our times will become one, and chronology will be lost in a world of meaningless symbols, and in some way it may be true to say that I once handed you this book and that you accepted it.

J.L.B.

Buenos Aires, 9 August 1960

[Preface to the 1964, 1966, and 1967 editions of *Obra poética*]

FOREWORD

This preface might be termed the aesthetics of Berkeley, not because the Irish metaphysician—one of the most lovable men in the whole history of philosophy—actually ever professed it, but because it applies to literature the same argument Berkeley applied to the outer world. The taste of the apple (states Berkeley) lies in the contact of the fruit with the palate, not in the fruit itself; in a similar way (I would say), poetry lies in the meeting of poem and reader, not in the lines of symbols printed on the pages of a book. What is essential is the aesthetic act, the thrill, the almost physical emotion that comes with each reading. Maybe there is nothing new in this, but at my age novelties matter far less than truth.

Literature's magic is worked on us by various artifices, but once the reader finds them out they wear off. Out of this comes the continual need for greater or lesser variations, which may recover a past or prefigure a future.

I have brought together in this volume all of my poetry except for certain exercises whose omission no one will regret or remark, and which (as Edward William Lane said of certain tales of *The Thousand and One Nights*) could not be purified without destruction. I have polished a few infelicities and pruned a certain excess of Hispanisms and Argentinisms, but in general I have resigned myself to the several Borges, or same Borges, of 1923, 1925, 1929, and 1960, and even to the Borges of 1964. This volume includes some hitherto unpublished pieces and a short appendix, or museum, of apocryphal poems.

As young poets are apt to do, I once believed that free verse is easier than regular verse; now I realize that free verse is more difficult, since it requires the inner conviction of many pages of Carl Sandburg or of his father, Whitman.

One of three fates awaits a book of poetry: it may be relegated to oblivion, it may not leave behind a single line and yet give a sufficient picture of the man who wrote it, or it may bequeath a few poems to the anthologist.

If the third were my case, I would like to survive in the "Conjectural Poem," in the "Poem of the Gifts," in "The Golem," and in "Limits." But all poetry is mysterious; nobody knows for sure what it has been given him to write. The dreary mythology of our time speaks of the subconscious or, what is even less lovely, of subconsciousness. The Greeks invoked the Muse, the Hebrews the Holy Ghost; the meaning is the same.

J.L.B.

Buenos Aires, 29 August 1964

[Preface to *Para las seis cuerdas* (1965)]

FOREWORD

All reading implies a collaboration and, in a sense, a complicity. If we want to enjoy Estanislao del Campo's *Fausto,* we must accept that a gaucho could possibly follow the plot of an opera sung in a language unknown to him; if we want to enjoy José Hernández' *Martín Fierro,* we must accept the unlikely succession of boasts and self-pity justified by the political aims of the writer but quite foreign to the hardy character of the gauchos and to the way a *payador* takes care not to offend an unknown audience.

In the humble case of my *milongas,* in place of the missing music the reader must imagine a man crooning to himself on his doorstep or in a corner saloon, and accompanying himself on the guitar. His hand seems to linger on the strings, and the words matter less than the tune.

I have done my best to avoid the sentimentality of the present-day tango and the artificial use of slang, which lends a spurious air to the simple lyrics.

As far as I am aware, these verses need no further explanation.

J.L.B.

Buenos Aires, June 1965

[Preface to *Seis poemas escandinavos* (1966)] *

What secret roads led me to the love of all things Scandinavian? Maybe the ties of blood, since my people on my father's side came from Northumberland, which once was Viking country. (This rather farfetched explanation is hardly sufficient; nobody yearns for what is already his.) Maybe a copy of the Völsunga Saga my father gave me about half a century ago, translated by William Morris and Eiríkr Magnússon into a kind of archaic, almost purely Saxon English. Maybe an impressive illustration in a history of the world—under their horned helmets, the Vikings, spears in hand, seemed to be looking me in the face, while in the background I could see the long ships with boldly striped sails belly-

---

* Privately printed by Gustavo Fillol Day in an edition of 84 copies (only 57 of which have been issued to date), with illustrations by Juan Carlos Benítez, Buenos Aires, 1966. The six poems are "Fragmento," "Hengest cyning," "A una espada en York" (not in the present selection), "Snorri Sturluson (1179–1241)," "A Carlos XII," "Emanuel Swedenborg."

ing out dramatically. Maybe the magic of certain words: Denmark, Norway, fjord, Odin, and Thor, the god of thunder, whose name survives in Thursday. Maybe the stiff and stubborn symbols of a runic alphabet. These things, of course, are guesswork. Later, there came Tacitus' *Germania,* whose compressed and difficult Latin I was once able to decipher; and the stormy figure of Charles XII, who swept Voltaire into epic writing; and the fiery prose of Thomas Carlyle. Still later, the discovery—even yet not clearly understood—that Germanic culture reached its flowering in Iceland, the Ultima Thule of the classical world. And later still, the fact (which I hope one day to pursue) that the first subjects in English literature were Scandinavian—Beowulf and Scyld and "the sixty men of victory in the battle of warriors." Then, the study of the medieval texts.

The epic is one of the necessities of the human mind. But with few exceptions—Lawrence of Arabia is one—it seems to have been forgotten by contemporary writers. Many people now search for the epic in Western movies and in their hard riders. More than in the Greeks and Romans and in the Lay of the Nibelungs, I have found the epic in the prose and poetry of the North. Hence, these poems.

I am not, by the way, the first intruder in the Spanish language to have explored such latitudes. Ricardo Jaimes Freyre's *Castalia bárbara* (1897), which contains these resounding verses, should not be overlooked:

> *Un Dios misterioso y extraño visita la selva.*
> *Es un Dios silencioso que tiene los brazos abiertos.*
>
> [A strange, mysterious God visits the forest.
> A silent God who stands with open arms.]

One final explanation. "Hengest Cyning" in Old English means "Hengest the King." He was, according to Bede, the first Germanic adventurer to found a royal line on English soil. He and his brother came from the north of Denmark.

J.L.B.

Buenos Aires, 14 December 1965

[Preface to *Siete poemas* (1967)] *

FOREWORD

There is something mysterious about the sonnet. Its form—two quatrains and two tercets of certain fixed line lengths, or, as practiced by Shakespeare, three quatrains and a rhymed couplet—may seem arbitrary, but throughout the centuries and across geography it has displayed a capacity for endless modulations. Any poem that follows the pattern of Manrique's elegy will never amount to more than an echo of Manrique, but a sonnet by Lugones does not remind us of one by Góngora, nor do the sonnets of Góngora remind us of those by Lope. Who does not immediately recognize the voice of Milton, Wordsworth, Rossetti, Verlaine, or Mallarmé?

I want to say something about my own efforts. I have been criticized for the poverty of my vocabulary and rhymes. I have deliberately sought such poverty. It is my belief that only common words can move us, and not those glibly provided by dictionaries; as to out-of-the-way rhymes, they merely distract, impede, or startle the reader. A stanza like

> *¡Qué descansada vida*
> *la del que huye el mundanal rüido*
> *y sigue la escondida*
> *senda, por donde han ido*
> *los pocos sabios que en el mundo han sido!*

seems to me more skillfully rhymed than

> *El jardín, con sus íntimos retiros,*
> *Dará a tu alado ensueño fácil jaula,*
> *Donde la luna te abrirá su aula*
> *Y yo seré tu profesor de suspiros.*†

whose studied sounds, of course, I cannot help but appreciate.

As to the following exercises, let them be judged by the reader. Abstract reasoning cannot improve a poem. Emerson has already remarked that arguments convince nobody.

J.L.B.

---

* Privately printed by Juan Osvaldo Viviano in an edition of 25 copies, with illustrations by Jorge Larco, Buenos Aires, 1967. The seven poems are "El sueño," "El mar," "Junín," "Una mañana de 1649," "Un soldado de Lee (1862)," "El laberinto," "Laberinto." (All but the first and last of these are in the present selection.)

† The first example is from Fray Luis de León's "Vida retirada," the second from Leopoldo Lugones' "Luna crepuscular." *Ed.*

[Preface to the 1969 edition of *Fervor de Buenos Aires*]

I have not rewritten this book. I have toned down its overwrought style, I have smoothed its rough spots, I have deleted sentimentality and imprecisions, and, in the course of this work, at times pleasant and other times merely uncomfortable, I have felt that that young man who wrote the book in 1923 was already essentially—what is the meaning of "essential"?—the elderly man who now resigns himself or else rewrites. We are the same person, both disbelieving either in failure or success or in literary schools and their dogmas, both fond of Schopenhauer, Stevenson, and Whitman. To my mind, *Fervor de Buenos Aires* foreshadows everything I was later to do. For what could be read between its lines, for what it somehow promised, Enrique Díez-Canedo and Alfonso Reyes generously gave it their approval.

Like the young men of 1969, those of 1923 were equally shy. Fearing their own inner poverty, they tried—as now—to hide it away under loud and innocent novelties. I, for example, set myself too many goals: to ape certain crudities (which I liked) in Miguel de Unamuno, to be a Spanish writer of the seventeenth century, to be Macedonio Fernández, to invent the metaphors already invented by Lugones, to celebrate a Buenos Aires of one-story houses, and—to the west or to the south—villas surrounded by iron fences.

At that time, I sought sunsets, the city's outer slums, and unhappiness; now I seek mornings, the downtown, and peace.

J.L.B.

Buenos Aires, 18 August 1969

[Preface to the 1969 edition of *Luna de enfrente* and *Cuaderno San Martín*]

Around 1905, the critic Hermann Bahr decided: "The one duty—to be modern." Some twenty-odd years later, I too took upon myself that quite superfluous obligation. To be modern is to be a contemporary, to be of the present. This is a fate we cannot avoid. Nobody—apart from a certain adventurer dreamed up by Wells—has discovered the art of living in the future or the past. There is no book which is not of its own time; the painstaking historical novel *Salammbô,* whose characters are mercenaries during the Punic Wars, is a typical nineteenth-century

French novel. The one thing we know for sure about Carthaginian literature, which may have been very rich, is that it could not have had a book like Flaubert's.

I also tried my hardest to be Argentine, oblivious of the fact that I already was. I went in for the risky acquisition of one or two dictionaries of local usage that gave me words whose meanings I can now hardly make out—*"madrejón," "espadaña," "estaca pampa,"* and so forth.

The city of *Fervor de Buenos Aires* always has something private about it; the city of this volume is rather ostentatious and public. I do not want to be unjust to this book. Certain pieces in it—"The Mythical Founding of Buenos Aires," "General Quiroga Rides to His Death in a Carriage" —perhaps contain all the dazzling beauty of a decalcomania; others— "Deathwatch on the Southside" is one—do not, I venture to say, dishonor the man who wrote them. The fact is that I feel removed from them; I take no responsibility for their mistakes or for their possible virtues.

I have made few changes in these two collections. They are no longer mine.

J.L.B.

Buenos Aires, 25 August 1969

[Dedication to the 1969 edition of *Luna de enfrente* and *Cuaderno San Martín*]

TO LEONOR ACEVEDO DE BORGES

I want to leave a written confession which at one and the same time will prove personal and general, since the things that happen to any man happen to all men. I am speaking of something now lost and far away— my earliest birthdays. I used to accept presents, thinking the whole while that I was no more than a child and that I had done nothing—absolutely nothing—to deserve them. Of course, I never spoke of this; childhood is an age of shyness. Since then, you have given me so many things, and the years and the memories are so many. Father; Norah; all four grandparents; your memories, and in them the memories of your forefathers— the patios, the slaves, the water seller, the charge of those Peruvian hussars, and the shame of Rosas—your honorable imprisonment, when so many of us men kept silence; the mornings in Montevideo, Geneva, and

Austin; the bright and dark times shared; your youthful old age; your love of Dickens and of Eça de Queirós—Mother, you yourself.

These words are just between us two, *et tout le reste est littérature,* as Verlaine, in his fine literary way, wrote.

J.L.B.

Buenos Aires, 7 October 1969

[Preface to *El otro, el mismo* (1969)]

Of my many books of verse, scribbled out of laziness, carelessness, and at times passion, *El otro, el mismo* is the one I prefer. Here are the "Poem of the Gifts," the "Conjectural Poem," "A Rose and Milton," "The Other Tiger," "Limits," and "Junín," which, if I am not led astray by partiality, do me no dishonor. Here also are my habits: Buenos Aires; the cult of my ancestors; the study of old Germanic languages; the contradiction of time, which passes, and of the ego, which lives on; my amazement that time—our substance—may be shared with others.

This book is no more than a compilation. The pieces in it wrote themselves not to make up a volume but out of different moods and occasions, so that the fact that each poem was written for its own sake accounts for certain monotonies of theme and for the repetition of words and maybe even of whole lines. In his literary circle on what was then Victoria Street, the writer—let's call him that—Alberto Hidalgo pointed out my habit of composing the same page, with slight variations, twice over. I now repent having answered him that he was no less binary, except that in his case the first version was somebody else's. Such were the regrettable manners of that time, which many people today look back on sentimentally. We were all doing our best to be the heroes of trivial anecdotes. Hidalgo was right; "Alexander Selkirk," * for example, does not greatly differ from "Odyssey, Book Twenty-three," and "The Dagger" foreshadows the *milonga* I have titled "A Knife on the Northside" * and maybe also my short story "The Meeting." What is strange, what I fail to understand, is that my second versions, like muffled, unwitting echoes,

* Not in the present selection. *Ed.*

[278]

are usually inferior to my first. Once, in Lubbock, on the edge of the Texas desert, a tall girl asked me whether on setting down "The Golem" I had not written a variation of "The Circular Ruins." I told her that I had traveled from the other end of the hemisphere in order to be handed that revelation, which was true. The two pieces do, however, have their differences: the short story is about the dreamer who is dreamed; the poem, which I wrote later, about the relationship between God and man, and perhaps between the writer and his work.

Man's languages are traditions that have something fatal about them. Individual experiments, in fact, amount to little, except when the innovator is content to evolve a museum piece—a game, like *Finnegans Wake* or Góngora's *Soledades,* designed for the discussion of literary historians or for mere notoriety. On occasion, I have been tempted into trying to adapt to Spanish the music of English or of German; had I been able to carry out that perhaps impossible adventure, I would be a great poet, like Garcilaso, who gave us the music of Italy, or like the anonymous Sevillian poet who gave us the music of Rome, or like Darío, who gave us that of Verlaine and Hugo. I never went beyond rough drafts, woven of words of few syllables, which very wisely I destroyed.

The fate of a writer is strange. At first, he is baroque—ostentatiously baroque—and after many years he may attain, if the stars are auspicious, not simplicity, which in itself is nothing, but a modest and hidden complexity.

Less than by any school, I have been educated by a library—my father's—and despite the vicissitudes of time and space, I believe I have not read those beloved volumes in vain. In the "Conjectural Poem," the influence of Browning's dramatic monologues is obvious; in others, the influence of Lugones and, I hope, of Whitman. On rereading these pages, I have felt closer to Modernism than to those later sects that were spawned by its decadence and that now deny it.

Pater wrote that all arts aspire to the condition of music, perhaps because in music meaning is form, since we are unable to recount a melody the way we can recount the plot of a story. Poetry, if we accept this statement, would be a hybrid art—the reduction of a set of abstract symbols, language, to musical ends. Dictionaries are to blame for this erroneous idea, for, as we seem to forget, they are artificial repositories, evolved long after the languages they explain. The roots of language are irrational and of a magical nature. The Dane who uttered the name of Thor or the Saxon who uttered the name of Thunor did not know whether these words stood for the god of thunder or for the noise that follows the lightning. Poetry tries to recapture that ancient magic. Without set rules, it works in a hesitant, daring manner, as if advancing in darkness. Poetry is a mysterious chess, whose board and whose pieces shift as in a dream and over which, after I am dead, I shall go on poring.

J.L.B.

Buenos Aires, 15 October 1969

[Translations by Norman Thomas di Giovanni
in collaboration with the author]

IV. SUPPLEMENT OF 1969 REVISIONS

Upon completion of *Elogio de la sombra* in June, 1969, Borges' publishers decided to divide the *Obra poética 1923–1967* into three parts and to issue a new edition of the author's poetry in four uniform, individual volumes. For this edition, Borges, the restless and habitual reviser of his poems, leaped at the opportunity to overhaul his work once more and to weed out some of the weaker pieces. The revisions were heaviest in *Fervor de Buenos Aires,* while in *El otro, el mismo* they were concerned almost exclusively with correcting misprints. I helped Borges with this work in all the volumes except *Fervor,* reading the texts to him, discussing the possible changes, and then taking down his dictation. I was nearly as eager to see this work done as he was because it afforded us the chance to set straight a large number of typographical and other errors that we had been catching and collecting over the months; many of these mistakes went back a number of years. Unfortunately, however, we were not in Buenos Aires to check final proof of most of this new edition, so that while a great deal in it was corrected, it also contains fresh mistakes of its own.

While we worked away, Borges in his characteristic humor spoke of our "disinfecting" the texts. Are these latest revisions definitive? Hardly. No sooner had we finished when Borges elatedly told a friend to be on the lookout for these new volumes because at last they were "just the way I want the poems to read." Then, suddenly bemused, he added, "For a while, at least."

It was too late to incorporate most of the revisions of Borges' early poems into the present book. At the time these revisions were made, nearly all of the early poems had already been translated. In the case of *Fervor de Buenos Aires*, new readers are possibly better served by the 1967 texts, which are closer in spirit to the originals, for much cutting and rewriting went into the 1969 revisions; nor do Borges' addition of two new poems ("The Southside" and "Rose") and appropriation of another ("Lines I Might Have Written and Lost Around 1922") from *El otro, el mismo* amount to much more than whims. This supplement lists all 1969 revisions not adopted in the texts of the present selection of poems. Only author's revisions and none of the fresh errors are taken into account. More information about these latest revisions is given on pp. 323–24.

FERVOR DE BUENOS AIRES *

Calle desconocida
  5. como una música esperada y antigua,
  6. como un grato declive.
  7. En esa hora en que la luz
     tiene una finura de arena,
  8. di con una calle ignorada,
 10. cuyas cornisas y paredes mostraban
 13. Todo—la medianía de las casas,
 14. las modestas balaustradas y llamadores,
 16. entró en mi vano corazón
 18. Quizá esa hora de la tarde de plata
19–20. diera su ternura a la calle,
 21. haciéndola tan real como un verso
     olvidado y recuperado.
22–26. [lacking]
 27. Sólo después reflexioné
 28. que aquella calle de la tarde era ajena,

* For change in order of texts, see p. 323.

29. que toda casa es un candelabro
30. donde las vidas de los hombres arden
    como velas aisladas,
32. camina sobre Gólgotas.

Inscripción sepulcral
Dedication. Para mi bisabuelo, el coronel Isidoro Suárez
 4. Impuso en la llanura de Junín
    término venturoso a la batalla
 8. Eligió el honroso destierro.
 9. Ahora es un poco de ceniza y de gloria.

Un patio
 3. Esta noche, la luna, el claro círculo,
 4. no domina su espacio.

Sala vacía
 6. de tiempo detenido en un espejo
 7. y ante nuestro examen se pierden
10. [lacking]
11–13. Desde hace largo tiempo
    sus angustiadas voces nos buscan
14. y ahora apenas están
16–22. La luz del día de hoy
    exalta los cristales de la ventana
    desde la calle de clamor y de vértigo
23. [lacking]
24–25. y arrincona y apaga la voz lacia

Rosas
 4. sobre la decente blancura
 6. alguien, como reproche cariñoso,
 7. pronunció el nombre familiar y temido.
12. como la sombra de una montaña remota
17. su nombre fue desolación en las casas,
19. y horror del tajo en la garganta.
21. porque son venales las muertes,
22. si las pensamos como parte del Tiempo,
31. un hecho entre los hechos
32. que vivió en la zozobra cotidiana
33. y dirigió para exaltaciones y penas

35. El mar, ahora, es una separación caudalosa
37. ya toda vida, por humilde que sea,

Remordimiento por cualquier defunción
5. de Quien deben negarse todos los predicados,
15. el caudal de las noches y de los días.

Inscripción en cualquier sepulcro
2. gárrulas transgresiones al todopoder del olvido,
3. enumerando con prolijidad
13. cuando tú mismo eres el espejo y la réplica

Ultimo resplandor
Title. Afterglow
2. por indigente o charro que sea,
6–7. cuando el sol último se ha hundido.
9. esa alucinación que impone al espacio
13. como cesan los sueños

Amanecer
2. que apenas contradicen los faroles
9. Curioso de la sombra
11. reviví la tremenda conjetura
19. sino inmortales como un bosque o un río,
20. la doctrina anterior
29. [lacking]
31. que erigen en compartida magia las almas,
36. y sólo algunos trasnochadores conservan,
37. cenicienta y apenas bosquejada,
38. la imagen de las calles
41. corre peligro de quebranto,
44. Pero de nuevo el mundo se ha salvado.

Despedida
4–5. [lacking]
7. Oh tardes merecidas por la pena,
9–14. campos de mi camino, firmamento
que estoy viendo y perdiendo . . .
15. Definitiva como un mármol
16. entristecerá tu ausencia otras tardes.

LUNA DE ENFRENTE

Casas como ángeles [lacking]

Mi vida entera
2. [lacking]
3. He persistido en la aproximación de la dicha y en la intimidad
   de la pena.
10. Creo que mis jornadas y mis noches
    se igualan en pobreza y en riqueza a las de Dios y a las
    de todos los hombres.

CUADERNO SAN MARTIN

A Francisco López Merino
13. la ardiente gravitación del amor—
14. los cargados minutos que justifican
15. esta abrumada vida.
21–22. en el que nos bendice el olvido.

EL OTRO, EL MISMO

El puñal
[follows "A un poeta sajón [II]"; for the present edition the author has
made a slight revision in the fifth paragraph]

Líneas que pude haber escrito y perdido hacia 1922
[lacking; moved to *Fervor de Buenos Aires,* where it follows "Despedida"]

El laberinto
[lacking; moved to *Elogio de la sombra,* where the lines are not capitalized]

NOTES

FERVOR OF BUENOS AIRES, pp. 1–29

"I wrote these poems in 1921 and 1922, and the volume came out early in 1923. The book was actually printed in five days; the printing had to be rushed, because it was necessary for us to return to Europe. . . . I had bargained for sixty-four pages, but the manuscript ran too long and at the last minute five poems had to be left out—mercifully. I can't remember a single thing about them. The book was produced in a somewhat boyish spirit. No proofreading was done, no table of contents was provided, and the pages were unnumbered. My sister made a woodcut for the cover, and three hundred copies were printed. In those days, publishing a book was something of a private adventure. I never thought of sending copies to the booksellers or out for review. Most of them I just gave away. I recall one of my methods of distribution. Having noticed that many people who went to the offices of *Nosotros*—one of the older, more solid literary magazines of the time—left their overcoats hanging in the cloak room, I brought fifty or a hundred copies to Alfredo Bianchi, one of the editors. Bianchi stared at me in amazement and said, 'Do you expect me to sell these books for you?' 'No,' I answered. 'Although I've written them, I'm not altogether a lunatic. I thought I might ask you to slip some of these books into the pockets of those coats hanging out there.' He generously did so. When I came back after a year's absence, I found that some of the inhabitants of the overcoats had read my poems, and a few had even written about them. As a matter of fact, in this way I got myself a small reputation as a poet." Jorge Luis Borges, "An Autobiographical Essay," in *The Aleph and Other Stories 1933–1969*, pp. 224–25.

UNKNOWN STREET, p. 3

Lines 1–2. De Quincey, in a footnote in his *Confessions of an English Opium-Eater* (*Collected Writings,* vol. III, p. 293), points out that "the Jews in elder times made two twilights, first and second: the first they called the dove's twilight, or crepusculum of the day; the second they called the raven's twilight, or crepusculum of the night." Borges has drawn attention to his mistake in at least three different editions of his poems, most recently in that of 1969.

SEPULCHRAL INSCRIPTION, p. 5

See p. 297, note on "A Page to Commemorate Colonel Suárez, Victor at Junín."

EMPTY DRAWING ROOM, p. 9

This poem is about a house Borges lived in on Bulnes Street in the early twenties; for another glimpse of shabby genteel family life in Buenos Aires, see "The Elder Lady" in *Doctor Brodie's Report*.

After six years (1810–1816) of fruitless military effort to incorporate the outlying provinces of the old Viceroyalty of the Río de la Plata—Uruguay, Paraguay, and Bolivia—the provinces of modern-day Argentina determined to declare their own independence from Spain. But as the jealousies and antagonisms deepened between liberal Buenos Aires intellectuals and the people of the interior, the search for a viable form of government became more and more elusive. The delegates to the 1816 Tucumán Congress, who signed the independence act, appointed an interim supreme dictator while they went about looking for a king. The supreme dictator ruled until 1819. Meanwhile, the power of local bosses, the caudillos, who held sway over their bands of gaucho cavalry (*montoneras*), had so increased that it soon became apparent that they would oppose king, dictator, or president. When, in 1819, congress drafted a highly centralist constitution, the provincial caudillos opposed it. The next fifteen years were fraught with disunity, chaos, and civil war. In this period, the two great factions rose: the Unitarians (*unitarios*), who favored a centralist government under Buenos Aires leadership; and the Federalists (*federales*), who demanded local autonomy and at the same time recognition by Buenos Aires of their rights in the national partnership. While the Unitarians, who included a large part of the wealthy and cultured families of Buenos Aires, were clear in their stand, the Federals were split between mutually suspicious provincial caudillos and the Buenos Aires party. Federalism, for each of these factions, proved to hold different meanings, and by the end of Rosas' reign it was little more than a cover for the self-serving sectionalism of the capital and the ranchers of Buenos Aires province.

Out of this upheaval of the 1820's, in the search for a man strong enough to crush all opposition, came Juan Manuel de Rosas. Born in 1793 of a leading Buenos Aires family, he grew up on the pampa on his father's ranch, of which he became manager at the age of sixteen. Competent, strict but just with his gauchos, by the age of twenty-five Rosas was a large landowner and cattle breeder, and by 1820 a powerful caudillo. With his small army, dressed by him in red (which became the color of the Federals), he began intervening in politics; in 1829, he marched on Buenos Aires to put down an uprising, and in the outcome he was installed as governor. As a result of intense political intrigue, Rosas had become the chosen instrument of a powerful group of landowners in the Province of Buenos Aires who were convinced that their well-being would be insured if control of the province and domination of the nation's major port were vested in their own number. Rosas' immediate policy was the punishment of his enemies and the demand of total submission to the Federal party. The purge of Unitarian army chiefs began; some were shot, others jailed, and the display of red ribbons on all persons became obligatory. His term up in 1832, Rosas refused re-election when the legislature would not extend his dictatorial powers, and for the next three years he dedicated himself to extending the borders of the province into Indian territory to the south and west of Buenos Aires. During this expedition, 6,000 hostiles were killed. Meanwhile, in the capital, Rosas' wife (according to certain sources) worked hard for his return; in an effort to stage an uprising, she founded a terrorist organization known as the *mazorca*. Three weak governors floundered in power, until at last the legislative council begged Rosas to return. He did—on his own terms: "total power . . . for as long as he thinks necessary." Installed again in 1835, for the next seventeen years Rosas ruled the country with an iron hand. The terror spread, and the dictator was proclaimed "Restorer of the Laws." In the streets, the *serenos* called out the hours with the chant, "Long live the Federation! Death to the savage Unitarians!" This was repeated in the press, from the pulpit, and in the schools. Of this terror, an American resident reported: "I have seen guards at mid-day enter the houses of citizens and either destroy or bear off the furniture . . . , turning the families into the streets, and committing other acts of violence too horrible to mention." In the marketplace, he continued, "Rosas hung the bodies of his many victims; sometimes decorating them in mockery, with ribands of the unitarian blue and even attaching to the corpses, labels, on which were inscribed the revolting words 'Beef with the hide.' " Ironically, though Rosas never took a grander title than Governor of Buenos Aires, his rule was far more centralist than the Unitarians had ever dreamed. In his foreign policy, Rosas engaged the country in a war with Bolivia (1837–39); intervened in the affairs of Uruguay throughout the 1830's and 40's; got himself into a costly war with France (1838–40); and suffered a blockade at the hands of an Anglo-French force (1845–48). Finally, by 1852, he had lost his support. A rival caudillo, with Brazilian and Uruguayan aid, marched upon Buenos Aires and defeated Rosas' Federals at Monte Caseros on February 3. Resigning as governor, the dictator fled and was carried into exile aboard a British warship. He settled on a small farm in Southampton, where he died in 1877; his remains have never been repatriated.

Both sides of Borges' family—to their everlasting credit—were staunch and active Unitarians. As the reader of these notes will find, several of them were deprived of their lives and fortunes, while others endured years of exile. The old discord went deep, and irrationality—or barbarism—still has its champions in present-day Argentina. Borges found it necessary to append the following paragraphs to the 1969 edition of *Fervor de Buenos Aires:*

> When I wrote this poem, I knew that one of my forefathers was a forefather of Rosas. There is nothing remarkable about this fact, given the scant population of the Argentine and the almost incestuous nature of our history.
>
> Back around 1922, nobody foresaw the present revisionism. This pastime consists of "revising" Argentine history, not in order to get at truth but in order to reach a foregone conclusion: the defense of Rosas or of any other convenient despot. I still am, as may be seen, a savage Unitarian.

GENERAL QUIROGA RIDES TO HIS DEATH IN A CARRIAGE, p. 35

Domingo Sarmiento has recorded that the leader of gauchos in the Argentine was

> a Mohammed who could change the dominant religion at will and set up a new one in its stead. He is omnipotent. His injustice is a misfortune for his victim, but it is not considered abuse, because the caudillo is permitted to be unjust; further, he must necessarily be unjust. He has always been so.

And when Sarmiento published his famous book, *Civilization or Barbarism,* in 1845, it was Juan Facundo Quiroga whom he had chosen as the central figure in his history and the man who best represented the ruthless figure of the caudillo.

Facundo Quiroga (1793–1835), known as the "Jaguar of the Plains," was born in La Rioja, and during the 1820's had extended his power over the eight-province region of the Andes. So cruel was his reputation (he typically ordered the throats cut of all prisoners who fell into his hands), so awesome was his presence, that he bred fear wherever he went. Although nominally a Federal, Quiroga became a threat and an annoyance to Rosas, and, in 1835, on his return to Córdoba from a meeting with Rosas in Buenos Aires, Quiroga was ambushed and murdered by the local ruling gang, the Reinafé brothers. Though Rosas was quick to order a costly funeral for the fallen general and to demand the death sentence for the assassins, it has always been believed that it was he who had arranged for Quiroga's death. Years later, from exile in England, Rosas wrote: "They say I ordered the assassination of the illustrious General Quiroga. But have they proved it?"

Borges has written about Quiroga in another poem, "Los llanos," also from *Luna de enfrente*. Some of its lines read:

> Over these plains Juan Facundo Quiroga unleashed an
>   empire made of lances.
> An outlaw empire, a poverty-ridden empire.
> An empire whose living drums were the hoofbeats of
>   mustangs beating a ruffle round humbled cities . . .
> An empire of the knife that feasts on waiting, trembling
>   throats. . . .

The present poem derives from the vivid account of what took place at Barranca Yaco in Part II, Chapter IX, of Sarmiento's *Facundo. Civilización y barbarie en las pampas argentinas* (as he later called it). Quiroga's coach was shot at and swarmed by a troop of gaucho militia with drawn sabers, who at once hacked the postilion and two or three others to pieces. The General then stuck his head out and asked for the commander of the party, ordering him to draw near. "What's the meaning of this?" asked Quiroga. For a reply he received a bullet in the eye that left him dead. Then Santos Pérez, who had shot Quiroga, repeatedly stabbed Quiroga's secretary with his sword. When the executions were finished, the carriage was drawn to the woods, filled with bodies. Even the horses were cut to pieces. A small boy remained alive. "Who's this boy?" asked Santos Pérez. A sergeant in the raiding party stepped forward and said: "This is my nephew; I answer for him with my life." Santos Pérez drew up to the man, shot him through the heart, quickly dismounted, and while the boy screamed, threw him to the ground and slit his throat.

In a piece called "Diálogo de muertos," collected in *El hacedor,* Borges has also imagined a conversation after death between Rosas and Quiroga.

MANUSCRIPT FOUND IN A BOOK OF
JOSEPH CONRAD, p. 37

Borges tells me that this poem had its origin in a practical joke played on him by Néstor Ibarra, who commissioned him to write a piece, to be used for advertising purposes, in which some tobacco product would be mentioned. Borges agreed on condition that he not be required to name any particular brand; following delivery, Ibarra paid him one or two hundred pesos. Later, when the poem was never used, Borges began to suspect his generous friend's joke.

DULCIA LINQUIMUS ARVA, p. 39

The title is from Virgil, Eclogue I, line 3:

> nos patriae finis et dulcia linquimus arua

> We depart from our own country, from the sweet
>   fields [of home]   (tr. Dudley Fitts)

Lines 1 and 6. The ancestors referred to here are the Acevedo and Suárez on Borges' maternal side. See in *Elogio de la sombra* the sonnet "Acevedo," on the town named for these settlers.

20. Isidoro Suárez.
21. Francisco Borges.

SUNSET OVER VILLA ORTÚZAR, p. 45

Villa Ortúzar was a poor neighborhood out by Buenos Aires' western cemetery (La Chacarita).

SAN MARTIN COPYBOOK, pp. 47–71

Borges has written that "the title has nothing to do with the national hero; it was merely the brand name of the out-of-fashion copybook into which I wrote the poems. . . ."

Line 8. Juan Díaz de Solis, looking for a passage to the Far East, entered the Río de la Plata (naming it El Mar Dulce, or Freshwater Sea) in February, 1516. On rowing ashore, he and his companions were killed and eaten by Indians—all within sight of his ships' crews. This probably took place on the Uruguayan bank. A town called Santa María de Buenos Aires was founded by Pedro de Mendoza at the beginning of 1535, but lasted only three years. The city was refounded in 1580 by Juan de Garay.

14–15. The Riachuelo is a small stream that marks the southern limits of Buenos Aires; the Boca del Riachuelo is a section of the city at the mouth of the stream.

20. The actual Palermo block where Borges grew up as a boy.

27. Hipólito Yrigoyen (1850–1933), a *Radical* politician, served as president from 1916–22; re-elected in 1928, he was ousted by General José Uriburu in 1930. Reference here is to the eve of the 1916 election.

28. José Saborido was an Uruguayan, who, while employed in the Buenos Aires customs, wrote some of the earliest tangos.

ISIDORO ACEVEDO, p. 53

Isidoro Acevedo (1828–1905), the author's maternal grandfather. Of him, Borges has recorded: "One day, at the age of nine or ten, he walked by the Plata Market. It was in the time of Rosas. Two gaucho teamsters were hawking peaches. He lifted the canvas covering the fruit, and there were the decapitated heads of Unitarians, with bloodstained beards and wide-open eyes. He ran home, climbed up into the grapevine growing in the back patio, and it was only later that night that he could bring himself to tell what he had seen in the morning. In time, he was to see many things during the civil wars, but none ever left so deep an impression on him."

Line 8. The Arroyo del Medio is the brook that marks the boundary between the provinces of Buenos Aires and Santa Fe. Adolfo Alsina (1829–1877), commander of civilian troops at Cepeda and Pavón, was an ardent partisan of autonomy for the Province of Buenos Aires, of which he was made governor in 1866; he also served as vice-president of the Republic in 1868.

12. Cepeda and Pavón were battles fought, respectively, in 1859 and

1861, in the civil wars that followed the downfall of Rosas. Buenos Aires lost the first and won the second. The battle of the Stockyard flats (los Corrales) was fought in 1880; again, it concerned the question of provincial autonomy.

34. Puente Alsina, another battle in the 1880 struggle.

DEATHS OF BUENOS AIRES, p. 61

La Chacarita is the vast western cemetery of Buenos Aires, opened to accommodate the victims of the yellow-fever epidemic of 1871, when 13,614 people died in six months. La Recoleta is the old northern cemetery, whose crypts are filled with Argentina's illustrious dead, including all of Borges' immediate ancestors. It is also, as Borges has noted in an earlier poem on this burial ground, "the place where I shall be buried."

Lines 35–36. These lines are from the "Milonga de Arnold." The next two read:

> La vida no es otra cosa
> Que muerte que anda luciendo.

Arnold was a convict, and he died in the prison colony in Tierra del Fuego, where he composed his poem.

38. *La Quema* is the municipal incinerator, located out by the cemetery.

61. Nuestra Señora del Socorro, a downtown church dating from the end of the eighteenth century.

73. Along these walls, Manuel Suárez, a sergeant major and a Unitarian, was executed by Rosas in 1842. He was Isidoro Suárez's brother.

A note by Borges which records certain details to do with the writing of the first part of the poem may be found on page 152 of *Poemas 1922–1943*.

TO FRANCISCO LOPEZ MERINO, p. 69

Francisco López Merino was a minor poet, born in La Plata in 1904, who committed suicide in 1928. He wrote musical and plaintive verses that reflected his interest in the French and Belgian symbolists. Borges, who had been a close friend of his, has written a second poem on his death; see "Mayo 20, 1928" in *Elogio de la sombra* (In Praise of Darkness).

THE CYCLICAL NIGHT, p. 79

Line 12. David Hume was brought into the poem in 1964. Originally, the line spoke of "The philologist Nietzsche," but after writing the poem Borges found that, long before Nietzsche, Hume had stated and justified the Stoic theory of cyclical time in the eighth of his *Dialogues Concerning Natural Religion* (1779).

25. Jerónimo de Cabrera, sixteenth-century Andalusian conquistador and founder, in 1573, of the Argentine city of Córdoba. General Miguel Estanislao Soler (1783–1849), fought in the Army of the Andes and at Ituzaingó, governed the Province of Montevideo, and served as minister to Bolivia; though a Federal, he was opposed to Rosas, and for a time lived in exile in Uruguay. For Laprida and Suárez, see, respectively, the notes on "Conjectural Poem" and "A Page to Commemorate Colonel Suárez, Victor at Junín."

CONJECTURAL POEM, p. 83

Francisco Narciso de Laprida was born in the western Argentine province of San Juan in 1786, studied in Chile, and received his law degree there in 1810. Returned to the city of San Juan the next year, where he practiced his profession, he was elected municipal magistrate (*alcalde*) in 1812. In the following years, he assisted in the support of San Martín's Army of the Andes, which was preparing to liberate Chile, and he was elected member and then president of the congress that met in Tucumán, in 1816, and declared the independence of the "United Provinces of South America." In 1824, he was representative of the Province of San Juan in the constituent assembly, meeting in Buenos Aires, of which he was made president. He was a signer of the 1826 constitution, but the next year, upon failure of the Unitarian cause (the constitution proved too centralist in spirit for the ruling caudillos), Laprida retired to San Juan. Under threat of persecution by Quiroga, he was eventually forced to flee to Mendoza, where he headed a small division in defense against invasion by the "Jaguar of the Plains." In 1829, Laprida found himself dug in against the Aldao forces; trying to escape after an attack in violation of an armistice, Laprida was hunted down and killed by a troop of gauchos. His body was never found.

José Félix Aldao (1785–1845) was one of three soldier brothers who fought for the independence of Chile under San Martín and later ruled their native province of Mendoza as caudillos. Beginning his career as a priest and chaplain to the army, Aldao ended with the rank of general and earned a reputation at the time of the events described in the poem as one of Rosas' most bloodthirsty followers.

Borges is related to Laprida through his maternal grandfather.

Lines 13–16. The captain is the Ghibbeline Buonconte of Montefeltro, who was killed in the defeat of Campaldino on 11 June 1289. See *Purgatorio*, V, 85–129. This same incident is the subject of Robert Lowell's sonnet "The Soldier" in *Lord Weary's Castle*. According to one questionable theory, Buonconte may have actually been killed by Dante, who fought in the battle and later bestowed immortality on the captain.

14. Cf. *Purgatorio*, V, 99:

> fuggendo a piede e sanguinando il piano.

A PAGE TO COMMEMORATE COLONEL SUAREZ, VICTOR AT JUNIN, p. 89

Isidoro Suárez (1799–1846), Borges' maternal great-grandfather. Born in Buenos Aires, Suárez began his army career in 1814 as a cadet in the Horse Grenadiers, and by 1816 was in Mendoza as part of the Army of the Andes, which was preparing to cross the cordillera to liberate Chile from Spanish domination. In the Chilean campaign, he fought at Chacabuco (February, 1817) and a few days later led a daring exploit, the capture in Valparaiso harbor of a Spanish brigantine of war, in which his force of fourteen soldiers and seven sailors overcame the ship's crew of 89. This won him advancement to second lieutenant. In 1818, he took part in the defeat of Cancha Rayada (March) and the victory of Maipú (April), acting with such gallantry in the latter battle that he was immediately promoted to first lieutenant. The next year, he fought at Bío-Bío and at Chillán, and, in 1820, embarked upon the Peruvian campaign, where, in December, he fought at Pasco—again with distinction—and was made captain. During the following two years he took part in at least six other actions, and again moved up in rank. In 1824, under Bolívar's command, Suárez became the hero of the day in the famous battle of Junín; he later fought at Ayacucho, and by the year's end had been promoted by Bolívar to colonel.

The War of Independence now over, Suárez remained in Peru another two years, until, accused of having been part of a conspiracy against Bolívar, he was exiled to Chile, from which he returned to Buenos Aires in 1827. There he was received with distinction, and, crossing over into Uruguay, he fought in the war against the Brazilian Empire. At this time, Suárez also became active in the Unitarian cause; in 1829, he fought at Las Palmitas, in the Province of Buenos Aires, where he defeated a minor Federal caudillo. The next year, when the Unitarians had lost power, he emigrated to Uruguay. In 1834, marrying into an old Uruguayan family, he settled on the land. He still continued to take part in the resistance against Rosas into the 1840's, but in ill health he retired to Montevideo, where he died. Suárez had been decorated more than twenty times. His remains were brought back to Argentina in 1879, and a town was named for him in the south of the Province of Buenos Aires.

The battle of Junín was fought in the highlands of Peru on 6 August 1824. The Royalist forces were made up of two cavalry units, totaling 1300 men; the Republicans, of a number of cavalry squadrons, numbering 900 men, under General Necochea. Two of these squadrons, the Hussars of Peru, were held in reserve back of a marshy stretch of land at the southern end of the battlefield. These reserve forces were commanded by the young Suárez. The Republicans were bottled up in a narrow pass between a hill on one side and a marsh cut by a stream on the other, and were thus unable to get out onto the open plain. It was five o'clock in the afternoon. Only two squadrons were able to meet the onrushing Royalists, and both of them were driven back. At this point, the second Republican general, Miller, began his attack; but his forces were also broken up. In the midst of this disorder and confusion, Necochea's trumpets sounded the call to reform, but his efforts were smashed by the Royalists, into whose hands he fell prisoner with a number of saber wounds. The air rang with the dry sound of steel against steel and the anger and cursing of men. Now from the marshes came Suárez's Hussars, attacking the Royalists from behind, cutting the enemy down with sabers and lances, and breaking their force. Encouraged by the spectacle, the rest of the Republican cavalry regrouped and from the front and flanks charged the regiments that Suárez was dispersing. Necochea was rescued; the battle lasted only forty-five minutes. The Royalist losses were 19 officers and 345 soldiers killed, and 80 taken prisoner;

the Republicans lost 3 officers and 42 soldiers, while 8 officers and 91 soldiers were wounded. Bolívar commended Suárez, saying that "when history describes the glorious battle of Junín . . . it will be attributed to the bravery and audacity of this young officer; as of today, you will no longer be the Hussars of Peru but will be called the Lancers of Junín."

Line 38. Cf. The opening line of Wordsworth's sonnet "The power of Armies is a visible thing . . ."

Borges has made use of events in his great-grandfather's life in at least two stories. See the first and next-to-last paragraphs of "The Life of Tadeo Isidoro Cruz (1829–1874)" in *The Aleph and Other Stories*. In "The Elder Lady," from *Doctor Brodie's Report,* Colonel Mariano Rubio's career parallels Suárez's almost exactly. Suárez's mother's maiden name, by the way, was Merlo y Rubio.

MATTHEW XXV: 30, p. 93

Matthew XXV: 30—"And cast ye the unprofitable servant into outer darkness: then there shall be weeping and gnashing of teeth."

Line 16. See Borges' commentary on "The Dead Man" in *The Aleph and Other Stories,* p. 271.

THE DAGGER, p. 95

Paragraph 2. Luis Melián Lafinur (1850–1939), Uruguayan historian distantly related to Borges. He was Colonel Borges' first cousin. Evaristo Carriego (1883–1912) was the popular Buenos Aires poet who, in Borges' words, "discovered the literary possibilities of the run-down and ragged outskirts of the city—the Palermo of my boyhood." He had been a neighbor of the Borges family, and in 1930 Borges published a book on him, *Evaristo Carriego.*

5. Tacuarembó is a town toward the north of Uruguay.

This poem, written during the last years of the Perón dictatorship, could not be published in the Argentine. Turned down by *La Nación* in an act of self-censorship, it finally appeared in Montevideo, in *Marcha,* on 25 June 1954. Borges used it the next year as a chapter in the second edition of his book on Carriego.

A SOLDIER OF URBINA, p. 101

Cervantes served as a private, in Italy, under Captain Diego de Urbina in 1571.

A SAXON, p. 107

The year 449 is given by Bede for the first Nordic invasion of England. This is Borges' earliest poem on a Saxon theme, and he now deeply regrets the slip of making his immigrant Saxon face the English climate unshod.

Line 17. Woden and Thunor are the Saxon names for Odin and Thor.
23–24. These are actual Saxon kennings.

See Borges' piece "The Witness" in Appendix II of the present volume.

THE GOLEM, p. 111

Joshua Trachtenberg, in *Jewish Magic and Superstition,* writes that the German Hasidim used "the word *golem* (literally, shapeless or life-less matter) to designate a homunculus created by the magical invocation of names, and the entire cycle of *golem* legends may be traced back to their interest."

Line 20. Though Judah Löw, the seventeenth-century Jewish rabbi from Prague, is credited with making the Golem, according to Trachten-berg the "legends of the *golem* were transferred . . . to R. Judah Löw b. Bezalel, without any historical basis." It turns out that John Hollander, the poem's translator, is a descendant of Rabbi Löw (or Loew); after making his translation, Hollander was inspired to write his own Golem poem, "Letter to Borges: A Propos of the Golem," which admirably complements the translation. Hollander's poem is printed in his book *The Night Mirror.*

39. Gershom Scholem is the distinguished Jewish scholar and author of *Major Trends in Jewish Mysticism.*

Borges' interest in the legend of the Golem dates from an early ac-quaintance with Gustav Meyrink's *Der Golem,* the first prose work in German Borges ever read. See Borges' article on "The Golem" in *The Book of Imaginary Beings,* pp. 112–14.

POEM OF THE GIFTS, p. 117

Borges was named Director of the Argentine National Library after the fall of Perón in 1955.

Line 27. Paul Groussac (1848–1929) had been a former director of the Biblioteca Nacional and was also a historian and critic whose prose style Borges has greatly admired. A short eulogy, written after Groussac's death, is collected in Borges' *Discusión*.

After writing the poem, Borges discovered that José Mármol, the nineteenth-century poet and novelist who directed the National Library until his death in 1871, had also gone blind.

CHESS, p. 121

The metaphor of life as a game of chess is to be found in the Rubáiyát, Stanza XLIX:

> 'Tis all a Chequer-board of Nights and Days
> Where Destiny with Men for Pieces plays:
>   Hither and thither moves, and mates, and slays,
> And one by one back in the Closet lays.

In his second edition, FitzGerald revised this to read:

> Impotent Pieces of the Game he plays
> Upon this Chequer-board of Nights and Days;
>   Hither and Thither moves, and checks, and slays;
> And one by one back in the Closet lays.

ELVIRA DE ALVEAR, p. 125

Elvira de Alvear (1907–1959) was a wealthy Argentine society woman and minor poet who lived for years in Paris, where she knew Valery Larbaud, James Joyce, and Alfonso Reyes. She and Borges were close friends for a long period. He wrote a preface to her poems in 1934.

Lines 3–5. Cf. Matthew IV: 8, "Again, the devil taketh him up into an exceeding high mountain, and sheweth him all the kingdoms of the world, and the glory of them;".

14. Ituzaingó, battle in the war against the Brazilian Empire, fought in

Uruguay, 20 February 1827. Elvira's great-grandfather, General Carlos de Alvear, led the victory.

The poem is reproduced on a bronze plaque on the Alvear family tomb in the Recoleta cemetery.

SUSANA SOCA, p. 127

Susana Soca (1906–1959) was an Uruguayan society woman and patron of the arts. She lived in Paris and also, in Montevideo, edited a magazine called *Entregas de la licorne*. She died in an airplane crash in Brazil.

THE OTHER TIGER, p. 129

The complete line from Morris runs:

> And the craft that createth a semblance, and fails of the
> heart's desire;

The source is *Sigurd the Volsung,* Book II, "Regina telleth Sigurd . . ." (*Collected Works of William Morris,* vol. XII, p. 76).

ALLUSION TO A SHADOW OF THE NINETIES, p. 133

Juan Muraña was one of the famous knife fighters of the old North-side of Buenos Aires before the turn of the century. He crops up in several of Borges' stories and poems. See "The Challenge" in *The Aleph and Other Stories* and "Juan Muraña" in *Doctor Brodie's Report.*

ALLUSION TO THE DEATH OF
COLONEL FRANCISCO BORGES, p. 135

Francisco Borges (1833–1874), the author's paternal grandfather, was born in Montevideo, and became an artillery cadet in 1850 during

Oribe's siege of the city. Two years later, he fought with an Uruguayan division at Caseros, when Rosas was overthrown. In 1855, moving to the Argentine, he offered "his arm and his sword to the government of the State of Buenos Aires." In 1857, he found himself a second lieutenant in the army of Colonel (later General) Emilio Mitre, and under Mitre's command he fought against the cacique Coliqueo in the battle of the Cañada de los Leones and, the next year, in a further expedition against the Indians.

From this point on, Borges took part in all the important battles (including Cepeda and Pavón) and many of the lesser engagements of the internecine civil wars between Buenos Aires province and the Argentine confederation, becoming captain in 1861 and sergeant major in 1863. In 1865, he fought in the war with Paraguay at Corrientes (25 May), Yatay (17 August), and Uruguayána (18 September); the next year, at Paso de la Patria and Itapirú (16–17 April), Estero Bellaco (2 May), Tuyutí (24 May), and Boquerón (16–18 July). He was wounded in each of these last two battles, the second time severely enough to force him into a long convalescence back in Buenos Aires, where he was promoted to lieutenant colonel. From February 1867 to the end of the year, he was back at the front; in 1868, he was made colonel. The next year, he was given command of the southern frontier of Buenos Aires, and in June 1870 he was sent to relieve caudillo López Jordán's siege of Paraná. There he met an Englishwoman, Frances (Fanny) Haslam, whom he married the next year. In this same year, 1871, Borges was made commander in chief of the northern and western frontiers of Buenos Aires and the southern frontier of Santa Fe, fighting in punitive expeditions against cattle-raiding Indians. In this capacity, he fought the important battle of San Carlos, 8 March 1872. The next year, Borges was back in Entre Ríos, putting down another rebellion by López Jordán, but by early 1874 he was able to return to his frontier outpost.

To this point, Borges was the professional soldier—"an object dragged from battle to battle," as described in one of his grandson's poems. Then, in the last year of his life, he became involved in a revolt against the government that was to force him into suicide. The 1874 elections became a test between Sarmiento, who, as president, could not succeed himself, and General Bartolomé Mitre (Emilio's brother), who had been president before Sarmiento and who had announced his new candidacy. Sarmiento, in control of patronage and the election machinery, was backing Nicolás Avellaneda, who was ultimately elected and inaugurated in October 1874. Meanwhile, Mitre had enlisted Borges' support for his revolution, which was to take place on October 12, expecting Borges to bring with him the troops at his command. When the government discovered the plot, Colonel Borges was summoned and asked what attitude he would assume in the conflict. "Until October 12," he said, "the government may count on my loyalty and on the troops entrusted to my honor." But events precipitated the revolt, and Borges, since he had given Sarmiento his word, found he could not fulfill his promises to his personal and political friends. Instead, he handed over his troops to the government and resigned his command. Misunderstanding his action, his friends branded him a traitor. On October 12, alone, Borges joined the uprising, putting himself as a private citizen under General Mitre's orders. The next month he was in command of a brigade, under Mitre, at the battle of La Verde (26 November). Toward the close of that day, Mitre ordered a retreat; Borges pointed out that the enemy was about to run out of fire power, but his judgment went unheeded. It was at this point, when the general repeated his order, that Borges mounted his horse and, accompanied by several of his loyal soldiers, slowly rode out, arms across his chest, toward the enemy lines. The revolt failed, Mitre was imprisoned for several months, but his life was spared. Borges died from his wounds two days later. In his last words, he said, "I have fallen in the belief of having fulfilled my duty and my convictions, and for the same principles that I have fought all my life."

In 1970, Jorge Luis Borges visited the battlefield at La Verde and saw the room at the *estancia* there where his grandfather died. He now plans a story around the colonel's moral conflict and the manner in which he met his death.

THE BORGES, p. 137

Lines 12–14 refer to Sebastian, king of Portugal (1554–1578), who, as a fanatical mystic, led an ill-fated crusade against the Mohammedans of northwest Africa. He and his army were annihilated in the desert, but many Portuguese refused to credit his death. Thereafter, "Sebastianism" became a religion, surviving until the beginning of this century in Portugal and Brazil. The career of this "hidden king" is reminiscent of that of Arthur in Britain and Olaf in Norway.

EMBARKING ON THE STUDY OF
ANGLO-SAXON GRAMMAR, p. 139

Line 3. The vast river is the Río de la Plata.

8. Haslam is the name of Borges' English ancestors.

9. "Last Saturday" refers to the first lesson Borges undertook in Anglo-Saxon, together with a handful of students, around 1956 or so. This incident is described in the author's "Autobiographical Essay."

9–10. "Julius Caesar . . . Britain": cf. the opening of the Anglo-Saxon Chronicle (The Parker Chronicle), "Sixty years before the Incarnation of Christ, the emperor Julius Caesar was the first of the Romans to invade Britain. . . ."

12. Reference is to one of the 95 riddles of the Exeter Book.

13. See Beowulf, lines 3171–3174.

TO A MINOR POET OF 1899, p. 151

The author had in mind an imaginary Modernist poet. In an earlier version, the date 1897 was given in the title. Borges later changed it for the obvious reason that 1899 was the year of his birth; in a playful way, he thereby makes himself into the minor poet of 1899.

HENGEST CYNING, p. 157

Hengest's story is told in the Anglo-Saxon Chronicle, beginning in the year 449; his name is also sometimes spelled "Hengist." "Cyning" is Anglo-Saxon for "king."

Lines 10–11. The Anglo-Saxon "gár-sceg" means both "spear-man" ("spear-warrior") and "ocean." According to Bosworth and Toller's *Anglo-Saxon Dictionary* (p. 362), "The myth of an armed man,—a spear-man is employed by the Anglo-Saxons as a term to denote the Ocean, and has some analogy to the personification of Neptune holding his trident. Spears were placed in the hands of the images of heathen gods. . . ."

FRAGMENT, p. 159

In the notes to *Seven Saxon Poems* (Plain Wrapper Press, 1972), Borges wrote: "This poem was written in Texas, in 1961. I had been struck by a strange experiment by the Bolivian poet Ricardo Jaimes Freyre, a sonnet of beauty and word music with no particular meaning. Using a quite different theme, I tried to do something similar in free verse. I have worked in a number of Saxon and Old Norse kennings."

TO A SAXON POET, p. 161

The poet addressed is the monk who composed "The Battle of Brunanburh," in which Irish Norsemen, Welsh, and Scots fought a combined army of Mercians and West Saxons in the year 937.
Line 3. Cf. "The Battle of Brunanburh," in line 14:

mǣre tungol,

SNORRI STURLUSON, p. 163

Snorri Sturluson (1179–1241), the Icelandic historian, mythologist, poet, jurist, statesman, and author of the Younger Edda and the *Heimskringla,* or *Stories of the Kings of Norway.*

TO CHARLES XII OF SWEDEN, p. 165

Charles XII (1682–1718), king of Sweden and, according to Voltaire, who wrote his biography, the most extraordinary man who ever lived.

EMANUEL SWEDENBORG, p. 167

Emanuel Swedenborg (1688–1772), Swedish scientist, philosopher, and visionary. He lived for many years in London, where he died.

EMERSON, p. 171

See Emerson's poem "Days."

RAFAEL CANSINOS-ASSENS, p. 179

Rafael Cansinos-Assens (1883–1964), Spanish poet, novelist, and prime mover of the ultraist movement. For his relationship with Borges, see Borges' "Autobiographical Essay" in *The Aleph and Other Stories,* pp. 221–22.

EVERNESS, p. 187

The word "everness" was coined by John Wilkins, the seventeenth-century English churchman and inventor of a universal philosophical language.

The title of the companion sonnet, "Ewigkeit," is German for "eternity."

OEDIPUS AND THE RIDDLE, p. 191

For other forms of the riddle, see Borges' article on "The Sphinx" in *The Book of Imaginary Beings,* pp. 211–12.

ANOTHER POEM OF GIFTS, p. 199

Line 12. Angelus Silesius, pseudonym of Johann Scheffler (1624–1677), German poet and mystic.

21. Reference is to the downfall of Perón in September 1955. On the sixteenth, there were army revolts in Córdoba, Rosario, Santa Fe, and Paraná; on the nineteenth, Perón resigned, fleeing the country aboard a Paraguayan gunboat; on the twenty-third, General Lonardi took power as provisional president.

47. *Gesta Dei per Francos* may be roughly translated as "Deeds of God done through the French." It was a medieval work.

59. Josiah Royce, illustrating the concept of infinity in *The World and the Individual* (1899), imagined a map of England that corresponded point for point with England itself. Consequently, it included the map, and within the map the map of the map ad infinitum. See Borges' piece "Of Exactitude in Science" in *A Universal History of Infamy.*

75. Frances Haslam (1845–1935) was Borges' English grandmother on his father's side and was Colonel Borges' wife. See the first chapter of Borges' "Autobiographical Essay."

ODE WRITTEN IN 1966, p. 205

Composed for the 150th anniversary of the declaration of independence of the Argentine confederation, which took place in Tucumán in 1816. President of the Tucumán Congress at that time was Francisco Narciso de Laprida. See note on "Conjectural Poem."

Lines 1–2. The rider is San Martín, whose equestrian statue stands in the Buenos Aires plaza named for him.

JUNÍN, p. 211

This Junín, named after the famous battle, is the town in the Province of Buenos Aires, some 150 miles west of the Argentine capital. Colonel Borges commanded the frontier outpost there in the early 1870's.

A MORNING OF 1649, p. 217

Charles I (1600–1649), king of Great Britain and Ireland, was beheaded on 30 January 1649 during the English civil wars. He refused to recognize the court that tried him, and on the scaffold said that he "did not believe the happiness of people lay in sharing government, subject and sovereign being clean different."

TO A SAXON POET, p. 219

The poet addressed this time is the unknown author of "The Wanderer."

Line 7. The allusion to pine trees is from Tacitus' *Germania.*

13. Cf. "The Wanderer," first half of line 5:

> wadan wræclāstas;

MILONGA OF THE TWO BROTHERS, p. 225

The *milonga* is a forerunner of the tango, dating from the 1870's. According to one authority, Ventura R. Lynch, it was invented by Buenos Aires hoodlums (*compadritos*) as a parody of Negro dances; Vicente Rossi, in his book *Cosas de negros,* claims the *milonga* originated out on the edges of Montevideo. The first *milongas* were danced.

Line 5. The Costa Brava was an area to the south of Buenos Aires, between Turdera and Lomas de Zamora, notorious for its tough inhabitants.

14. The Iberras were five brothers from Lomas de Zamora, the most infamous of whom was Julio. There is a brief article on this family in Borges' anthology *El compadrito,* second edition (1968), pp. 65–67.

MILONGA OF ALBORNOZ, p. 229

Alejo Albornoz was a Buenos Aires hoodlum, who was actually knifed around 1902 or 1903. His story was told to Borges by an old police captain, don José Olave. Many details in the poem have, of course, been altered.

THE GENEROUS ENEMY, p. 241

Magnus Barfod was king of Norway from 1094 to 1103. His story is told in the *Heimskringla,* but the letter from Muirchertach is a fiction. Magnus was called "Barefoot" (or "Bareleg") for having brought back from Scotland and Ireland the custom of wearing the kilt.

The poem is made up of a number of Norse kennings, which Borges has willfully bestowed on the Irish king.

TO COLONEL FRANCISCO BORGES, p. 247

Line 5. Manuel Oribe was the Uruguayan caudillo, allied with Rosas, who besieged Montevideo for nine years (1843–52). Colonel Borges began his military career at the age of sixteen or seventeen during this siege.

8. Borges was wounded in two different battles in 1865 during the war with Paraguay.

9. Ricardo López Jordán was the Entre Ríos caudillo who laid siege to Paraná around 1870. Colonel Borges was sent to relieve the city.

10. Catriel, Pampas Indian cacique in the southwest of the Province of Buenos Aires; Martín Fierro, the hero of José Hernández' poem. Colonel Borges commanded the frontier outpost at Junín in the early 1870's.

See also note above on "Allusion to the Death of Colonel Francisco Borges."

THE MAKER, p. 256

See Borges' comment on this piece in *The Aleph and Other Stories,* pp. 277–78.

A YELLOW ROSE, p. 257

Giambattista Marino (1569–1625), Italian baroque poet whose avowed purpose was to astonish the reader with farfetched metaphors and skillfully melodious verses. His contemporary worshipers considered him superior to Dante and Homer.

The verses are from *L'Adone,* III, 158, lines 1–2:

> Porpora de' giardin, pompa de' prati,
> Gemma di primavera, occhio d' aprile,

EVERYTHING AND NOTHING, p. 259

Beginning of second sentence in last paragraph, cf. Job XXXVIII: 1, "Then the Lord answered Job out of the whirlwind, and said,".

BORGES AND MYSELF, p. 260

See the author's comment in *The Aleph and Other Stories,* pp. 276–77.

CONTENTS OF THE PRINCIPAL EDITIONS OF BORGES' POETRY

A. FERVOR DE BUENOS AIRES

Fervor de Buenos Aires. Privately printed by the author. Buenos Aires, 1923. Cover woodcut by Norah Borges. 7⅜ x 5¼ inches. 64 pages, unnumbered. Approximately 300 copies.

A quien leyere [preface]
1. Las calles
2. La Recoleta
3. Calle desconocida
4. El Jardín Botánico
5. Música patria
6. La plaza San Martín
7. El truco
8. Final de año
9. Ciudad
10. Hallazgo
11. Un patio
12. Barrio reconquistado
13. Vanilocuencia
14. Villa Urquiza
15. Sala vacía
16. Inscripción sepulcral [I]
17. Rosas
18. Arrabal
19. Remordimiento por cualquier defunción
20. Jardín
21. Inscripción en cualquier sepulcro

22. Dictamen
23. La vuelta
24. La guitarra
25. Resplandor
26. Amanecer
27. El Sur [I]
28. Carnicería
29. Alquimia
30. Benarés
31. Alba desdibujada
32. Judería
33. Ausencia
34. Llaneza

35. Llamarada
36. Caminata
37. La noche de San Juan
38. Sábados
39. Cercanías
40. Caña de ámbar
41. Inscripción sepulcral [II]
42. Trofeo
43. Forjadura
44. Atardeceres
45. Campos atardecidos
46. Despedida

B. *LUNA DE ENFRENTE*

Luna de enfrente. Proa. Buenos Aires, 1925. Five unsigned woodcut decorations by Norah Borges. 11½ x 9⅝ inches. 44 pages. 300 copies, numbered 1–300. *This is the scarcest of all the author's books.*

al tal vez lector [preface]
47. calle con almacén rosao
48. al horizonte de un suburbio
49. los llanos
50. antelación de amor
51. dualidá en una despedida
52. el general Quiroga va en coche al muere
53. jactancia de quietud
54. Montevideo
55. a Rafael Cansinos-Assens
56. singladura
57. apuntamiento de Dakar
58. la promisión en alta mar
59. tarde cualquiera

60. la vuelta a Buenos Aires
61. dulcia linquimus arva
62. a la calle Serrano
63. casi Juicio Final
64. casas como ángeles
65. mi vida entera
66. último sol en Villa Ortúzar
67. para una calle del Oeste
68. patrias
69. soleares
70. por los viales de Nîmes
71. el año cuarenta
72. en Villa Alvear
73. versos de catorce

C. CUADERNO SAN MARTIN

Cuaderno San Martín. Proa. Buenos Aires, 1929. Frontispiece pencil drawing of the author by Silvina Ocampo. 8½ x 6¼ inches. 64 pages. 280 copies as follows: 250 copies on featherweight paper, numbered 1–250; 10 copies on rag paper, numbered I–X; 20 copies on pure laid rag paper, lettered [Spanish alphabet] A to Q (not for sale).

74. La fundación mitológica de Buenos Aires
75. Arrabal en que pesa el campo
76. Elegía de los Portones
77. Fluencia natural del recuerdo
78. Isidoro Acevedo
79. La noche que en el Sur lo velaron
80. A la doctrina de pasión de tu voz
81. Muertes de Buenos Aires
82. A Francisco López Merino
83. Barrio Norte
84. El Paseo de Julio
    Anotaciones [notes]

D. POEMAS [1922–1943]

Poemas [1922–1943]. Losada. Buenos Aires, 1943. Cover drawing by A. Rossi. 8¼ x 6 inches. 184 pages. 2,500 copies.

Reprinted from *A. Fervor de Buenos Aires:* (a) a revised version of the last paragraph only of "A quien leyere" (see note on p. 269); (b) all but eight of the poems. **Rejected** are Nos. 5, 9, 10, 22, 31, 35, 40, 41. **Retitled** are No. 25 to "Ultimo resplandor" and No. 32 to "Judengasse". **Revised texts:** preface and all the poems. **Extent of revisions:** minor (affecting a tenth or less lines), Nos. 15, 33, 42, 46; moderate (affecting more than a tenth and less than a third lines), Nos. 1, 4, 7, 17, 20, 26, 27, 29, 30, 31, 37, 43; extensive (affecting a third or more lines), Nos. 2, 3, 6, 8, 11, 12, 13, 14, 16, 18, 19, 21, 23, 24, 25, 28, 34, 36, 38, 39, 44, 45.

Reprinted from *B. Luna de enfrente:* all but eight of the poems. **Rejected** are the preface and Nos. 59, 60, 62, 68, 69, 70, 71, 72. **Retitled** are No. 47 to "Calle con almacén rosado", No. 50 to "Amorosa anticipación", and No. 57 to "Dakar". **Revised typography:** (a) titles no longer printed in lower-case letters; (b) lines of verse no longer all capitalized. **Revised texts:** all the poems. **Extent of revisions** (not counting the typographical revision and the correction of a large number of typographical errors, including printer's substitution—apparently he had run out of type—of the letter "I" for "Y"): minor, Nos. 47, 50, 53, 54, 61, 64, 65; moderate, Nos. 48, 49, 51, 52, 57, 63, 66, 67; extensive, Nos. 55, 56, 58, 73.

Reprinted from *C. Cuaderno San Martín:* (a) all the poems but one; (b) notes. **Identical with previous printing:** No. 80. **Rejected:** No. 75. **Revised texts:** all the poems except No. 80 and, very slightly, the notes. **Extent of the revisions** (not counting matters of printer's styling and the correction of inconsistent indenting of first lines in stanzas): minor, Nos. 74, 76, 77, 78, 79, 81, 82, 84; moderate, No. 83.

Added to *Luna de enfrente* section, following, respectively, Nos. 54 and 55:

85. Al coronel Francisco Borges   86. Manuscrito hallado en un libro
    (1833–1874)   de Joseph Conrad

Added in new final section, *Otros poemas:*

87. Prose poems for I.J.   90. Del infierno y del cielo
88. Insomnio   91. Poema conjetural
89. La noche cíclica   Notas [notes]

E. POEMAS 1923–1953

Poemas 1923–1953. Emecé. Buenos Aires, 1954. 7⅜ x 5 inches. 176 pages. 3,000 copies.

Reprinted from *D. Poemas [1922–1943]:* all texts except for one poem. **Rejected:** No. 14. **Retitled:** No. 87 to "Two English Poems". **Identical with previous printing:** (a) preface to *Fervor;* (b) Nos. 1, 3, 4, 6, 7, 11, 13, 15, 16, 18, 19, 20, 24, 27, 28, 30, 32, 34, 38, 39, 42, 43, 44, 45, 46, 47, 48, 49, 50, 51, 54, 56, 57, 61, 63, 64, 65, 66, 67, 73, 77, 79, 83, 84, 86, 87, 88, 90. **Revised texts:** (a) minor, Nos. 2, 8, 17, 21, 25, 33, 36, 37, 52, 53, 55, 58, 74, 76, 78, 80, 81, 82, 85, 89, 91; moderate, Nos. 12, 23; extensive, Nos. 26, 29; (b) slight revisions in both sets of notes, except that one long note of 4½ pages dropped from second set. **Revised order of texts:** No. 8 follows 15, 16 follows 7, 11 follows newly ordered 16. **Added:** (a) epigraph from Robert Louis Stevenson; (b) to final section, retitled *Otras composiciones:*

92. Poema del cuarto elemento
93. A un poeta menor de la Antología

94. Página para recordar al coronel Suárez, vencedor en Junín
95. Mateo XXV, 30

F. *POEMAS 1923–1958*

Poemas 1923–1958. Emecé. Buenos Aires, 1958. 7⅜ x 5 inches. 184 pages. 3,000 copies.

Reprinted from *E. Poemas 1923–1953:* preface to *Fervor* and all but one of the poems. **Rejected:** (a) No. 32; (b) all the notes. **Identical with previous printing:** Nos. 1, 3,* 7, 11,* 12, 16, 18, 20, 21, 23,* 25, 26, 28, 29, 30, 33, 36, 37, 38,* 39, 42, 43, 44, 46, 54, 55, 56, 57, 61, 63,* 64, 65, 66, 67, 74, 77,* 81,* 82,* 83, 85, 86, 87,* 88,* 89, 90,* 91, 93, 94,* 95. **Revised texts:** (a) preface to *Fervor;* (b) minor, Nos. 2, 6, 13, 15, 17, 19, 24, 27, 34, 45, 47, 48, 49, 50, 51, 52, 58, 73, 76, 78, 79, 80, 84, 92; moderate, Nos. 4, 8, 53. **Added** to *Otras composiciones:*

96. Una brújula
97. Una llave en Salónica
98. Un poeta del siglo XIII
99. Un soldado de Urbina
100. Límites [I]

101. Baltasar Gracián
102. Un sajón (A.D. 449)
103. El Golem
104. El tango

G. *From EL HACEDOR*

El hacedor. Emecé. Buenos Aires, 1960. 7⅜ x 5 inches. 116 pages. 5,000 copies.

A Leopoldo Lugones [preface]
105. Poema de los dones

106. El reloj de arena
107. Ajedrez
108. Los espejos

* Except for obvious typographical error(s).

109. Elvira de Alvear	121. A Luis de Camoens
110. Susana Soca	122. Mil novecientos veintitantos
111. La luna	123. Oda compuesta en 1960
112. La lluvia	124. Ariosto y los árabes
113. A la efigie de un capitán de los ejércitos de Cromwell	125. Al iniciar el estudio de la gramática anglosajona
114. A un viejo poeta	126. Lucas, XXIII
115. El otro tigre	127. Adrogué
116. Blind Pew	128. Arte poética
117. Alusión a una sombra de mil ochocientos noventa y tantos	129. Cuarteta †
	130. Límites [II] †
118. Alusión a la muerte del coronel Francisco Borges (1835–74)	131. El poeta declara su nombradía †
	132. El enemigo generoso †
119. In memoriam A. R.	133. Le regret d'Héraclite †
120. Los Borges	

H. OBRA POÉTICA 1923–1964

Obra poética 1923–1964. Emecé. Buenos Aires, 1964. Frontispiece drawing of the author by Héctor Basaldúa; eight color illustrations, two each, by Héctor Basaldúa, Norah Borges, Horacio Butler, and Raúl Soldi. 8⅛ x 5⅞ inches. 284 pages. 3,000 copies.

Reprinted from *F. Poemas 1923–1958:* all texts but one of the poems. **Rejected:** No. 29. **Retitled:** No. 27 to "Sur" and No. 74 to "Fundación mítica de Buenos Aires". **Identical with previous printing** (neither here nor in the following list of revisions is note made of those dropped accents in single-syllable words adopted in conformity with new Spanish-language rules): (a) preface to *Fervor;* (b) Nos. 3,* 7, 12, 13, 18, 19, 20, 21, 24, 34, 42, 43, 44, 46, 48, 53, 58, 63, 77, 78,* 81,* 83, 87,* 88,* 90,* 91, 92, 94,* 95,** 96, 97, 98, 99, 102. **Revised texts:** minor, Nos. 4, 6, 11, 15, 26, 27, 30, 33, 36, 37, 38, 47, 52, 61, 67, 74, 76, 79, 80, 82, 84, 85, 86, 89, 100, 101, 103, 104; moderate, Nos. 1, 2, 8, 16, 17, 23, 25, 28, 39, 45, 50, 51, 54, 56, 57, 64, 65, 66, 73, 93; extensive, Nos. 49, 55. **Revised order of texts:** No. 87 follows 88.

† Grouped under the heading *Museo.*
* Except for obvious typographical error(s) or correction of error(s) from previous printing.
** Title slightly revised to read "Mateo, XXV, 30".

Reprinted from *G. El hacedor:* "A Leopoldo Lugones" and all verse texts. **Identical with previous printing:** Nos. 105, 106, 109, 110, 112, 113, 114, 116, 117,* 118, 119, 120, 121, 123,* 127, 128, 130, 131,* 133. **Revised texts:** (a) "A Leopoldo Lugones" (very slight); (b) minor, Nos. 107, 108, 111, 115, 124, 125, 126; moderate, Nos. 122, 129, 132.

Added to opening of volume, following epigraph:
Prólogo [foreword]

Added to *Otras composiciones,* now retitled *El otro, el mismo,* and following No. 128:

134. El otro
135. Una rosa y Milton
136. Lectores
137. Juan, I, 14 [I]
138. El despertar
139. Buenos Aires [I]
140. A quien ya no es joven
141. Alexander Selkirk
142. Odisea, libro vigésimo tercero
143. El
144. Milonga de dos hermanos †
145. ¿Dónde se habrán ido? †
146. Sarmiento
147. A un poeta menor de 1897
148. Texas
149. Composición escrita en un ejemplar de la Gesta de Beowulf
150. Fragmento
151. A un poeta sajón [I]
152. Hengest cyning
153. E. A. P. (1809–49)
154. Everness
155. Ewigkeit
156. Edipo y el enigma
157. Spinoza
158. España
159. Elegía
160. Adam Cast Forth
161. A una moneda
162. Otro poema de los dones

Revised order of texts: "A Leopoldo Lugones" prefaces *El otro, el mismo* section; Nos. 129, 130, 131, 132, 133 follow No. 162 in a new final section, *Museo.*

I. PARA LAS SEIS CUERDAS

Para las seis cuerdas. Emecé. Buenos Aires, 1965. Eleven illustrations by Héctor Basaldúa. 14¼ x 10¼ inches. 60 pages, unnumbered. 3,015

---

* Except for obvious typographical error(s) or correction of error(s) from previous printing.
† Grouped under the heading "Dos letras de milonga."

copies as follows: 3,000 ordinary copies; 15 copies on cream-white paper, numbered I–XV, with a set of illustrations and an original by the artist on white paper.

Reprinted from *H. Obra poética 1923–1964:* Nos. 139, 144, 145. **Revised texts:** minor, Nos. 144, 145; moderate, No. 139.

The volume opens with a
     [foreword]
and, following No. 145, these new texts:

163. Milonga de Jacinto Chiclana
164. Milonga de don Nicanor Paredes
165. Un cuchillo en el Norte
166. El Títere
167. Alguien le dice al tango
168. Milonga de los morenos
169. Milonga para los orientales
170. Los compadritos muertos

J. OBRA POÉTICA 1923–1966

Obra poética 1923–1966. Emecé. Buenos Aires, 1966. 7⅜ x 5 inches. 336 pages. 3,000 copies.

Reprinted from *H. Obra poética 1923–1964:* all texts but one of the poems. **Rejected:** No. 24. **Retitled:** No. 147 to "A un poeta menor de 1899" and No. 153 to "Edgar Allan Poe". **Identical with previous printing:** (a) foreword; (b) preface to *Fervor;* (c) Nos. 3, 4, 7, 11, 12, 13, 15, 16, 17, 18, 19, 20, 21, 25, 26, 27, 28, 30, 37, 38, 39, 43, 44, 45, 46, 47, 48, 49, 50, 51, 52, 53, 54, 55,* 56, 57, 58, 61, 63, 64, 65, 66, 67, 73, 74, 76, 77, 78, 79, 80, 81, 82, 83, 84, 85, 86, 87, 88, 89, 90, 92, 93, 94, 95, 96, 97, 98, 99, 100, 101, 102, 103, 104, 105, 106, 107, 108, 109, 110, 111, 112, 113, 114, 116, 117, 118, 119, 120, 121, 123, 125, 126, 127, 128, 129, 130, 131, 132, 133, 134, 135,* 136, 137,* 138, 140, 141, 142, 143, 145, 146, 147, 148, 149, 150, 151,* 152, 153, 154, 155, 156, 157, 158, 159, 160, 161, 162; (d) "A Leopoldo Lugones." **Revised texts:** minor, Nos. 1, 2, 6, 33, 34, 36, 42, 91, 115, 122, 124, 139, 144; moderate, Nos. 8, 23.

Reprinted from *I. Para las seis cuerdas:* all texts. **Identical with previous printing:** (a) foreword; (b) Nos. 165,* 167, 168. **Revised texts:** minor, Nos. 163, 166, 169, 170; moderate, No. 164.

* Except for obvious typographical error.

Added to *El otro, el mismo,* following No. 150:
171. A una espada en York

Added following No. 151:
172. Snorri Sturluson (1179–
1241)
173. A Carlos XII
174. Emanuel Swedenborg

175. Jonathan Edwards (1703–
1758)
176. Emerson

Added following No. 153:
177. Camden, 1892
178. París, 1856
179. Rafael Cansinos-Assens
180. Los enigmas
181. El instante
182. Al vino
183. Soneto del vino

184. 1964
185. El hambre
186. El forastero
187. A quien está leyéndome
188. El alquimista
189. Alguien

Added following No. 162:
190. Oda escrita en 1966

191. Líneas que pude haber
escrito y perdido hacia 1922

Added to *Para las seis cuerdas,* following No. 169:
192. Milonga de Albornoz

Revised order of texts: No. 152 follows 149, 170 follows 191; Nos. 144 and 145, together with Nos. 163, 164, 165, 166, 167, 168, 169, 192 form a new section (with its own foreword), *Para las seis cuerdas,* which follows *El otro, el mismo* and precedes *Museo.*

K. OBRA POETICA 1923–1967

Obra poética 1923–1967. Emecé. Buenos Aires, 1967. 7⅜ x 5 inches. 340 pages. 5,000 copies.

Reprinted from *J. Obra poética 1923–1966:* all texts but three of the poems. **Rejected:** Nos. 55, 80, 85. **Identical with previous printing** (not counting printer's errors committed in the process of offsetting from the previous edition or similar errors corrected from previous edition): all texts but for one poem. **Revised text:** moderate, No. 52.

Added to *El otro, el mismo,* following No. 191:

193. El sueño	198. Buenos Aires [II]
194. Junín	199. A un poeta sajón [II]
195. Un soldado de Lee (1862)	200. Al hijo
196. El mar	201. El laberinto
197. Una mañana de 1649	

L. From *ELOGIO DE LA SOMBRA*

Elogio de la sombra. Emecé. Buenos Aires, 1969. Endpaper and frontispiece color illustrations by Héctor Basaldúa. 9¼ x 7⅛ inches. 164 pages. 6,000 copies, the first of which, numbered I and signed by the author, bears the original illustrations.

[preface]	216. Israel
202. Juan, I, 14 [II]	217. Junio, 1968
203. Heráclito	218. El guardián de los libros
204. Cambridge	219. Los gauchos
205. Elsa	220. Acevedo
206. New England, 1967	221. Milonga de Manuel Flores
207. James Joyce	222. Milonga de Calandria
208. The Unending Gift	223. Invocación a Joyce
209. Laberinto	224. Israel, 1969
210. Mayo 20, 1928	225. Dos versiones de "Ritter,
211. Ricardo Güiraldes	Tod und Teufel"
212. A cierta sombra, 1940	226. Buenos Aires [III]
213. Las cosas	227. Fragmentos de un evangelio
214. Rubáiyát	apócrifo
215. A Israel	228. Un lector
	229. Elogio de la sombra

Included from *El otro, el mismo* section of *K. Obra poética 1923–1967,* following No. 208: No. 201.

M. FERVOR DE BUENOS AIRES

Fervor de Buenos Aires. Emecé. Buenos Aires, 1969. Endpaper and color frontispiece illustration by Norah Borges. 9¼ x 7⅛ inches. 162 pages. 3,000 copies, the first of which, numbered I and signed by the author, bears the original illustrations.

Reprinted from *Fervor de Buenos Aires* section of *K. Obra poética 1923–1967:* (a) "A quien leyere"; (b) all but three of the poems. **Rejected:** Nos. 4, 13, 27. **Retitled:** No. 25 to "Afterglow". **Identical with previous printing:** (a) "A quien leyere" and (b) No. 28. **Revised texts:** minor, Nos. 6, 34, 43, 45; moderate, Nos. 11, 17, 19, 21, 26, 37, 39, 42; extensive (affecting from one-third to two-thirds lines), Nos. 8, 12, 15, 16, 18, 20, 23, 25, 36, 38, 44; rewritten (affecting two-thirds or more lines), Nos. 1, 2, 3, 7, 30, 33, 46. **Revised order of texts:** No. 8 follows 17, 11 follows 7, 28 follows newly ordered 8, 39 follows 37. **Added** to opening and close of volume, respectively:

[preface]   Notas [notes]

Added following Nos. 2 and 16, respectively:
230. El Sur [II]   231. La rosa

Included from *El otro, el mismo* section of *K. Obra poética 1923–1967,* following No. 46: No. 191.

N. LUNA DE ENFRENTE and CUADERNO SAN MARTIN

Luna de enfrente y Cuaderno San Martín. Emecé. Buenos Aires, 1969. Endpaper and color frontispiece illustration by Juan Eichler. 9¼ x 7⅛ inches. 138 pages. 3,000 copies, the first of which, numbered I and signed by the author, bears the original illustrations.

Reprinted from *Luna de enfrente* and *Cuaderno San Martín* sections of *K. Obra poética 1923–1967:* all but one of the poems. **Rejected:** No. 64. **Retitled:** No. 51 to "Una despedida". **Identical with previous printing:** Nos. 57, 76,* 77, 84,* 86.* **Revised texts:** minor, Nos. 52, 56, 66, 67, 74, 78,* 79,* 81 *; moderate, Nos. 48, 49,* 50, 58, 73,* 82,* 83;

* Except for obvious typographical error(s) or correction of error(s) from previous printing.

extensive, Nos. 47, 53, 54, 61, 63, 65; rewritten, No. 51. **Added** to opening of volume:

A Leonor Acevedo de   [preface]
Borges [dedication]

O. EL OTRO, EL MISMO

El otro, el mismo. Emecé. Buenos Aires, 1969. Endpaper and frontispiece color illustrations by Raúl Soldi. 9⅛ x 7 inches. 274 pages. 3,000 copies, the first of which, numbered I and signed by the author, bears the original illustrations.

Reprinted from *El otro, el mismo, Para las seis cuerdas,* and *Museo* sections of *K. Obra poética 1923–1967:* (a) "A Leopoldo Lugones"; (b) foreword to *Para las seis cuerdas;* and (c) all but three of the poems. **Rejected:** No. 167. **Transferred** to other volumes: No. 191 to *M. Fervor de Buenos Aires* and No. 201 to *L. Elogio de la sombra.* **Retitled:** No. 171 to "A una espada en Yorkminster". **Title corrected:** No. 118, "Alusión a la muerte del coronel Francisco Borges (1833–74)". **Identical with previous printing:** (a) foreword to *Para las seis cuerdas;* (b) Nos. 88, 90,* 91,* 92, 93, 94,* 95, 96, 97, 98, 99, 100,* 101,* 102,* 104,* 105,* 106, 108, 109,* 110, 112, 113, 114, 115,* 117,* 118, 119, 120, 121, 122, 123,* 125,* 126, 127,* 128,* 129,* 130, 131,* 132,* 133, 136, 137, 138, 139, 140, 141, 142, 143, 144,* 145,* 146, 147, 148, 149, 150, 151, 152,* 153, 154, 155, 156,* 157, 158, 159,* 160, 161, 162,* 163, 164,* 165, 166, 168,* 169,* 170,* 171, 172, 173, 174, 175,* 176, 177,* 178, 179, 180,* 181, 182, 183, 184,* 185, 186, 187, 188,* 189, 190,* 192, 193,* 194, 195, 196,* 197, 198, 199, 200. **Revised texts:** (a) "A Leopoldo Lugones" (slight); (b) minor, Nos. 87,* 89,* 103,* 107, 111, 116, 124,* 134, 135. **Added** to opening of volume: [preface]

Added, following No. 200:
232. El puñal

* Except for obvious typographical error(s) or correction of error(s) from previous printing.

INDEX OF SPANISH AND ENGLISH TITLES

A Carlos XII, 164
Adam Cast Forth, 194
Adam Cast Forth, 195
A Francisco López Merino, 68
Afterglow, 19
Ajedrez, 120
Alba desdibujada, 250
Al coronel Francisco Borges (1833–1874), 251
Alguien, 184
Al iniciar el estudio de la gramática anglosajona, 138
Allusion to a Shadow of the Nineties, 133
Allusion to the Death of Colonel Francisco Borges (1833–1874), 135
Along the Byways of Nîmes, 249
Alusión a la muerte del coronel Francisco Borges (1833–74), 134
Alusión a una sombra de mil ochocientos noventa y tantos, 132

Amanecer, 20
Amorosa anticipación, 32
A Morning of 1649, 217
Another Poem of Gifts, 199
Anticipation of Love, 33
A Page to Commemorate Colonel Suárez, Victor at Junín, 89
A Poet of the Thirteenth Century, 99
A quien está leyéndome, 182
A quien ya no es joven, 146
A Rafael Cansinos-Assens, 252
A Rose and Milton, 145
Ars Poetica, 143
Arte poética, 142
A Saxon (A.D. 449), 107
A Soldier of Urbina, 101
A Soldier Under Lee (1862), 213
At the Butcher's, 25
A una moneda, 196
A un poeta menor de la Antología, 86
A un poeta menor de 1899, 150

A un poeta sajón [I], 160
A un poeta sajón [II], 218
A Yellow Rose, 257

Blurred Dawn, 246
Borges and Myself, 260
Borges y yo, 266

Calle desconocida, 2
Camden, 1892, 174
Camden 1892, 175
Carnicería, 24
Carved on a Tombstone, 247
Casas como ángeles, 40
Chess, 121
Compass, 97
Composición escrita en un ejemplar de la Gesta de Beowulf, 154
Conjectural Poem, 83
Cuarteta, 234

Daybreak, 21
Deaths of Buenos Aires, 61
Deathwatch on the Southside, 57
Despedida, 28
Dulcia Linquimus Arva, 38
Dulcia Linquimus Arva, 39

Edgar Allan Poe, 172
Edgar Allan Poe, 173
Edipo y el enigma, 190
El enemigo generoso, 240
El general Quiroga va en coche al muere, 34
El Golem, 110
El hacedor, 261
El laberinto, 220
El mar, 214
El otro tigre, 128
El poeta declara su nombradía, 238
El puñal, 94
El Sur, 253
El testigo, 264
Elvira de Alvear, 124
Elvira de Alvear, 125

Emanuel Swedenborg, 166
Emanuel Swedenborg, 167
Embarking on the Study of Anglo-Saxon Grammar, 139
Emerson, 170
Emerson, 171
Empty Drawing Room, 9
Everness, 186
Everness, 187
Everything and Nothing, 264
Everything and Nothing, 259
Ewigkeit, 188
Ewigkeit, 189

Fragment, 159
Fragmento, 158
Fundación mítica de Buenos Aires, 48

General Quiroga Rides to His Death in a Carriage, 35

Hengest cyning, 156
Hengest Cyning, 157
Houses Like Angels, 41

Inscripción en cualquier sepulcro, 16
Inscripción sepulcral [I], 4
Inscripción sepulcral [II], 251
Inscription on Any Tomb, 17
Isidoro Acevedo, 52
Isidoro Acevedo, 53

Jonathan Edwards (1703–1758), 168
Jonathan Edwards (1703–1758), 169
Junín, 210
Junín, 211

La noche cíclica, 78
La noche que en el Sur lo velaron, 56
La rosa, 254
Límites [I], 102
Límites [II], 236
Limits, 103
Limits (or Good-byes), 237
Líneas que pude haber escrito y perdido hacia 1922, 208

Lines I Might Have Written and Lost
    Around 1922, 209
Llaneza, 26
Los Borges, 136
Los enigmas, 180
Lucas, XXIII, 140
Luke XXIII, 141

Manuscript Found in a Book of Jo-
    seph Conrad, 37
*Manuscrito hallado en un libro de
    Joseph Conrad*, 36
Mateo, XXV, 30, 92
Matthew XXV:30, 93
Milonga de Albornoz, 228
Milonga de dos hermanos, 224
Milonga of Albornoz, 229
Milonga of the Two Brothers, 225
Mi vida entera, 42
Muertes de Buenos Aires, 60
My Whole Life, 43

Oda escrita en 1966, 204
Ode Written in 1966, 205
Odisea, libro vigésimo tercero, 148
Odyssey, Book Twenty-three, 149
Oedipus and the Riddle, 191
Otro poema de los dones, 198

*Página para recordar al coronel Suá-
    rez, vencedor en Junín*, 88
París, 1856, 176
Paris 1856, 177
Parting, 29
Patio, 7
Plainness, 27
Poema conjetural, 82
Poema de los dones, 116
Poem of the Gifts, 117
Poem Written in a Copy of Beowulf,
    155
Por los viales de Nîmes, 253

Quatrain, 235

Rafael Cansinos-Assens, 178

Rafael Cansinos-Assens, 179
*Remordimiento por cualquier defun-
    ción*, 14
Remorse for Any Death, 15
Rosas, 10
Rosas, 11
Rose, 250

Sala vacía, 8
Sepulchral Inscription, 5
Snorri Sturluson (1179–1241), 162
Snorri Sturluson (1179–1241), 163
Someone, 185
Spinoza, 192
Spinoza, 193
Sunset Over Villa Ortúzar, 45
Susana Soca, 126
Susana Soca, 127

Texas, 152
Texas, 153
The Borges, 137
The Cyclical Night, 79
The Dagger, 95
The Enigmas, 181
The Generous Enemy, 241
The Golem, 111
The Labyrinth, 221
The Maker, 256
The Mythical Founding of Buenos
    Aires, 49
The Other Tiger, 129
The Poet Tells of His Fame, 239
The Sea, 215
The Southside, 249
The Witness, 258
To a Coin, 197
To a Minor Poet of 1899, 151
To a Minor Poet of the Greek An-
    thology, 87
To a Saxon Poet [I], 161
To a Saxon Poet [II], 219
To Charles XII of Sweden, 165
To Colonel Francisco Borges (1833–
    1874), 247

To Francisco López Merino, 69
To My Reader, 183
To One No Longer Young, 147
To Rafael Cansinos-Assens, 248
Two English Poems, 75

Ultimo resplandor, 18
Ultimo sol en Villa Ortúzar, 44
Una brújula, 96

Una mañana de 1649, 216
Una rosa amarilla, 263
Una rosa y Milton, 144
Unknown Street, 3
Un patio, 6
Un poeta del siglo XIII, 98
Un sajón (A.D. *449*), 106
Un soldado de Lee (1862), 212
Un soldado de Urbina, 100

THIS BOOK WAS SET IN TIMES ROMAN

BY BROWN BROTHERS LINOTYPERS, INC.,

PRINTED BY HALLIDAY LITHOGRAPH CORPORATION,

AND BOUND BY AMERICAN BOOK-STRATFORD PRESS, INC.

DESIGNED BY JOEL SCHICK